ONE HUNDRED
VIOLENT
FILMS
THAT CHANGED CINEMA

NEIL FULWOOD

B T BATSFORD

For Alex Thompson

AUTHOR'S NOTE

This book focuses on 100 films that have had an effect on the portrayal of violence in cinema, be it in terms of influence, iconography, social response, media controversy or censorship. In order to provide context, it has been necessary to mention a number of other films. Therefore, the 100 films under specific discussion are identified in the text in **boldface**.

All stills courtesy of The Joel Finler Picture Collection, except for those on pages 63 and 112, which are from the author's own collection.

First published 2003
© Neil Fullwood 2003
The right of Neil Fulwood to be identified as the author of this work has been asserted by him in accordance with the Copyright, Designs and Patents Act 1988.

ISBN 0 7134 8819 0
A CIP catalogue record for this book is available from the British Library.

Printed in Spain by Just Colour Graphics S. L.
for the publishers
B T Batsford Ltd
64 Brewery Road
London N7 9NT
www.batsford.com
A member of **Chrysalis** Books plc

Distributed in the United States and Canada by Sterling Publishing Co., 387 Park Avenue South, New York, NY 10016, USA

CONTENTS

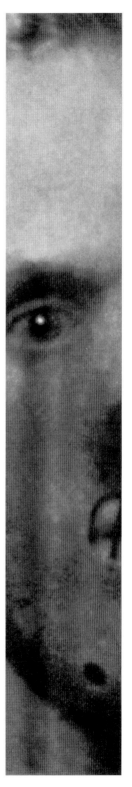

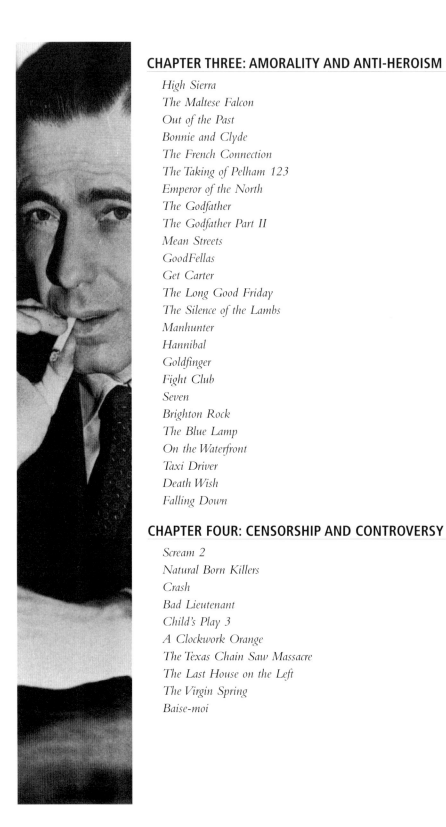

CHAPTER THREE: AMORALITY AND ANTI-HEROISM   47

CHAPTER FOUR: CENSORSHIP AND CONTROVERSY   81

influence and iconography

CHAPTER ONE

Midway through **Die Hard** (John McTiernan, 1988), the lone, outnumbered hero John McClane (Bruce Willis) shares his first exchange with his antagonist Hans Gruber (Alan Rickman) via two-way radio. Gruber asks him who he is and, when no answer is forthcoming, sneeringly calls him 'just another American who saw too many movies as a child, another orphan of a bankrupt culture who thinks he's John Wayne, Rambo, Marshall Dillon.'

'Actually, I was always partial to Roy Rogers,' McClane wisecracks. 'I really dug those sequinned shirts.'

It's a witty exchange, one of several highly quotable sections of dialogue in this top-notch action film, but it's also very telling. Cinema – particularly American cinema – is keyed into itself, conscious of its own traditions and iconography in a way that perhaps no other form of mass entertainment is.

Bruce Willis as John McClane in *Die Hard*

Die Hard is a perfect example of the development of one of American cinema's most popular characters: the maverick, lone-wolf hero. John McClane embraces a tradition that stretches back through the nonconformist, rule-breaking cops of the Seventies (*Dirty Harry*, *The French Connection*), larger-than-life, seemingly indestructible Sixties icons (James Bond and his ilk), hard-bitten, roll-with-the-punches protagonists of Forties and Fifties film noir, to the cowboy heroes referenced in McClane and Gruber's conversation. Clearly, an interchangeability of genre conventions exists in mainstream cinema. And when one begins to analyze the subject of movie violence, it soon becomes evident that many of the key films are easily defined by genre: action thriller, crime/gangster, horror, western.

The western is a good place to start. Not only does it contain the traditions that *Die Hard* and any number of pyrotechnic blockbusters so gleefully embrace, but also it is the quintessential American genre, and one whose popularity has been inextricably linked with one of the key American icons.

Clint Eastwood and the development of the western

He was destined from the start to epitomize the western. As Rowdy Yates in the long-running television series *Rawhide*, Clint Eastwood became a household name. But it was his role as the Man With No Name in Sergio Leone's 'Dollars' trilogy that turned him into an icon.

For a genre so steeped in American history (or at least its myths and folklore), it is ironic that the filmmaker who single-handedly redefined the western (muddying the lucid morality of John Ford and Anthony Mann) and made Eastwood into a megastar in the process was Italian[1]. Even more so when one considers that their first collaboration, ***A Fistful of Dollars*** (1964), is a remake of a Japanese film, *Yojimbo* (Akira Kurosawa, 1961)[2].

No Name is an appropriate appellation, one that could just as well be No History (we learn nothing of his background), No Qualms (he kills without compunction) or No Morality (he plays off prospective paymasters against each other for his own financial benefit). As the title suggests, he answers only to cold, hard cash. His methods are brutal; violence, distributed by gun and fist, becomes the film's *raison d'être*. Leone protracts the tension deliberately, building up to fast-edited, noisy shoot-outs, then has No Name dismissively walk away from the carnage.

The character's mercenary tendencies are even further to the fore in *For a Few Dollars More* (1965). Such narrative as there is centres on No Name joining forces with bounty hunter Colonel Mortimer (Lee Van Cleef) to rob a Mexican bandit (Gian Maria Volonté). Everyone is ruthless, obsessed with material gain. No-one flinches from the use of brute force. Leone's stylizations detract from an emotionless premise and make the film an exercise in iconography.

The final instalment of the trilogy, ***The Good, the Bad and the Ugly*** (1966), marks the apogee of the spaghetti western, and points Eastwood towards his later, self-directed westerns. Eastwood is again joined by Van Cleef (this time playing an assassin called Angel

Eyes) and are the good and bad respectively, with Eli Wallach rounding out the cast (and stealing the movie) as Tuco, a Mexican bandit who is most assuredly the ugly.

Again, financial motivations are at the forefront. No Name and Tuco run a scam whereby No Name turns his partner in, collects the reward money and then engineers Tuco's escape by shooting the rope before he can be hanged. Meanwhile, Angel Eyes, learning from one of his victims of a cashbox buried beneath an unmarked grave, sets out to claim the loot for himself.

The Tuco/No Name partnership degenerates when greed rears its ugly head:

> **Tuco:** The neck at the end of the rope is mine. I run the risks. So next time, I want more than half.
> **No Name:** You run the risks, my friend, but I do the cutting. You cut down my percentage, it might interfere with my aim.
> **Tuco:** But if you miss, you had better miss very well.

No Name and Tuco are soon in opposition to each other and to Angel Eyes. What follows is as mercenary as in the previous films, and as violent: Angel Eyes kills two men and slaps around a woman in order to identify the last owner of the cash box; later he watches with barely concealed pleasure as Tuco, incarcerated in a prison camp, is bloodily beaten by a burly jailer. Not that Tuco's suffering elicits much sympathy, the bandit having robbed and humiliated a gunsmith and made several attempts on the life of his former partner. He later takes revenge on the jailer, killing the man as he hurls him from a moving train.

Development, however, is in the humanizing of No Name's character. Of the three leads, he is the most frugal in his recourse to violence, even sparing Tuco at the end when he has him at his mercy. In the film's most epic scene of civil war conflict – a battle between opposing battalions for a strategically worthless bridge – No Name opines, 'I've never seen so many men wasted so badly.'

This element of *The Good, the Bad and the Ugly*, its wartime backdrop, also distances it from its predecessors, Leone demonstrating not just humanity but political awareness[3]. The futility and brutality of war are well demonstrated. The entrenchments around the bridge provide a metaphor for the trench warfare of the World War I, while the inhumanity on display at the camp (Tuco's beating is poignantly

The Man With No Name: Clint Eastwood in *The Good, the Bad and the Ugly*

juxtaposed with an elegiac threnody played by imprisoned musicians) brings to mind the concentration camp atrocities of World War II. From this maelstrom, No Name emerges not as the emotionless cipher of the first two films, but as a man made weary by the violence he sees around him.

There followed a couple of pedestrian westerns which played on Eastwood's amoral No Name persona – *Hang 'Em High* (Ted Post, 1968) and *Joe Kidd* (John Sturges, 1972) – as well as two very different ones for Don Siegel, the comedic *Two Mules for Sister Sara* (1970), and the dark psycho-sexual drama *The Beguiled* (1971). Then, in 1973, he made **High Plains Drifter**, his second film as director and his first self-directed western. It fuses the stylish compositions of Leone and the psychological darkness of *The Beguiled*. Eastwood plays the Stranger, the personification of a community's guilt at the murder of their sheriff. For all the acts of violence (and rape) that the Stranger doles out, punishing not only those who participated but those who stood and watched, it is the flashbacks to the sheriff's death that provide the most visceral moments of violence: outnumbered and unable to loose off a single shot against his tormentors, he is whipped to death. The scene is protracted – indeed, it unfolds over the course of several flashbacks.

If the violence in *High Plains Drifter* is graphic and unpleasant, and the plot merely an excuse for a revenge drama, it is Eastwood's

11

approach to the material that makes it more than just another spurs-and-six-guns potboiler. A dream-like quality often pervades the film; its *mise-en-scènes* are coloured by a surrealism more akin to Lynch than Leone. During his tenure, the Stranger deposes the mayor and appoints a dwarf, Mordecai (Billy Curtis), in his place, then orders the town to be painted red and renames it 'Hell'. Riding out of town, his vengeance complete, his final words are spoken with Mordecai, busy carving a headstone: 'I never did know your name,' Mordecai says. 'Yes, you do,' the Stranger replies. A close-up of the headstone shows the dead sheriff's name.

Still, notwithstanding aesthetic development and the emergence of a personal vision, the casual portrayal of violence in *High Plains Drifter* does not represent any sense of evolvement from the Leone films. **The Outlaw Josey Wales** (1976), however, is a complete reappraisal of the western. Wales (played by Eastwood himself) begins the film as peaceable farmer, a family man, content not to become swept up in the civil war as long as he can work his piece of land. This is not to be. Marauding Confederate troops sack and set fire to his homestead, killing his wife and son and leaving him badly beaten. He joins a Rebel outfit and rides against them.

Finding himself on the losing side at the surrender, Wales refuses to join his comrades in swearing allegiance to the Union. A wise decision, since they are promptly mown down by a Gatling gun in a massacre orchestrated by the sadistic Captain Tirrell (Bill McKinney). After staging a retributive attack of his own, Wales heads for Texas, an outlaw, pursued by bounty hunters whose number includes his former comrade Fletcher (John Vernon). Already, Wales is clearly established as a character forced into violence by war, injustice and betrayal.

As the film develops, it becomes less about Wales's flight from his pursuers as his attempt to find a safe haven for the ersatz family he gains: the group of settlers he saves from robbery and rape; the old Indian chief whose lands have been lost to the white man; the squaw he rescues from the abusive owner of a trading post. He determines to live in peace, but the world isn't content to let him be. In one of the film's most celebrated scenes, a gunslinger goes up against him in a bar:

> **Wales:** You a bounty hunter?
> **Gunslinger:** A man's got to do somethin' for a livin' these days.
> **Wales:** Dyin' ain't much of a livin', boy. [Pause] You know, this isn't necessary. You can just ride on.

Wordlessly, the man walks away. Barely have Wales's companions been able to exhale before the bounty hunter re-enters. 'I had to come back,' he says ruefully. 'I know,' Wales replies – and proves himself the faster on the gun. Again, the emphasis is not on quick-draw heroics, but the sad inevitability of a pointless death.

Eastwood's anti-violence message is reiterated at the denouement. Wales leads his 'family' to an idyllic spot, makes peace with the Indian tribe who inhabit that territory and establishes a settlement. Still, it is not long before Tirrell and his men track them down. Tirrell's mob is defeated and Wales finally confronts Tirrell himself. In a potent metaphor, Wales pulls no less than four guns as he advances, the hammer falling on empty chambers each time, before dispatching Tirrell with his own cavalry sword. Eastwood's intent couldn't be better illustrated: *The Outlaw Josey Wales* is a western about peace and unity, a western that rejects the gun.

A decade later, Eastwood revisited the vaguely supernatural premise of *High Plains Drifter*. The biblically titled *Pale Rider* (1985) begins with the Preacher (so called because he wears the clothes of priest, never mind that he dishes out beatings and uses a revolver in a manner not mentioned anywhere in the Good Book) appearing as if in answer to the prayers of a young girl whose family, part of a community of miners, are being run off their land by a ruthless businessman who wants to muscle in on their claims.

If the Preacher is a throwback to *High Plains Drifter* (angel of vengeance instead of vengeful reincarnation), the difference here is motive. The Stranger takes revenge on a township, the Preacher defends one. As with *Josey Wales*, violence is done for the preservation of values – community, unity, the right to live and work in peace.

Eastwood brought the cycle to a close in 1992 with his (at the time of writing) last western, the Oscar-winning **Unforgiven**. His character, William Munny, is not too dissimilar from No Name. In fact, he could be the No Name of *The Good, the Bad and the Ugly* nearly 30 years down the line, his conscience fully developed and steeped in remorse.

Munny is a former gunslinger who turned his back on 'drink and wickedness' for the love of a decent woman. But time has passed and age has crept up on him. His wife has died and the responsibility for their two children has fallen to him. His dirt farm is a failure; his herd of swine are dying of fever. So when a young braggart, the Scofield Kid (Jaimz Woolvett), offers him a part of the bounty on two

Clint Eastwood as ageing gunslinger William Munny in *Unforgiven*

cowpokes responsible for attacking a prostitute, the monetary considerations prove too great and he allows himself to be dragged back into his old profession. He ropes in his former partner, Ned (Morgan Freeman), and the three set off for the town of Big Whiskey and a double killing.

What follows is a western that works on the level of Jacobean tragedy. The morality of violence is debated in almost every scene. The cowboys have already been punished by the law – in the form of Messianic sheriff 'Little' Bill (Gene Hackman) – threatened with a whipping and obliged to make financial reparations. The 'girls' at the brothel where the attack occurred (sparked off by a discouraging laugh at one of the men's under endowment) pool their resources to post a bounty, an act that attracts flamboyant gunslinger English Bob (Richard Harris). Travelling with his own biographer (Saul Rubinek), a writer of lurid folkloric 'histories', Bob is savagely kicked along Main Street by 'Little' Bill for refusal to conform to local ordnance and surrender his weapon.

Staying on after his employer has been run out of town, Bob's biographer solicits a more accurate account of the west from 'Little' Bill. Eastwood uses these scenes both to demythologize the genre (quick-draw contents are revealed as farcical events, guns jamming or blowing up in their owners' hands) and to humanize Bill's character. Initially portrayed as a sadist with a badge, he is revealed as a man who just wants to build a house, sit on the porch and enjoy the sunset. Violence is a tool of his job, necessary for the discouragement of 'assassins and men of low character'.

Violence scars everybody's lives. Both the cowboys die badly: one slowly and painfully (he crawls out of range and Munny is unable to administer the *coup de grâce*), the other ignominiously as he squats in an outhouse. The 'girls' are rounded on and treated heavy-handedly by pimp/brothel-owner Skinny, himself pressured by Bill over the influx of bounty hunters into Big Whiskey. The Scofield Kid, for all his big talk, is left almost physically sick by the act of killing:

Scofield Kid: It don't seem real, how he'll never breathe again, ever. How he's dead.
Munny: It's a hell of a thing, killin' a man. To take away everything he's got and everything he's gonna have.
Scofield Kid: Yeah. Well, I guess they had it coming.
Munny: We all have it coming, kid.

Ned is captured and dies during interrogation under Bill. Munny reverts to his old ways, polishing off a bottle of whisky and riding into town to settle the score. The transition is chilling in its swiftness – the suggestion being that this is who Munny really is, that the years of sobriety and non-aggression have been merely a facade. He as much as admits this when he faces Bill down:

Bill: You'll be William Munny out of Missouri, killed women and children.
Munny: That's right. I've killed women and children. Killed just about anything that walked or crawled at one time or another. Now I'm here to kill you, Little Bill, for what you did to Ned.

Munny is left alive at the end of the film, a coda informing us that he and his children left the dirt farm for 'San Francisco where it was rumoured he prospered in dry goods'. Morally, this is a more dangerous conclusion than if he had died in Big Whiskey: not only has his reversion to violence (at which he has proved very proficient) been profitable, but also he has made no payment for his sins.

If *Unforgiven* does prove to be Eastwood's valediction to the genre (thematically, one is left with that impression), it is a complex and challenging one, and a fitting summation by a filmmaker whose contribution to the development of the western is equalled only by that of Sam Peckinpah – a man whose name has become synonymous with cinematic violence.

The aesthetics of violence

When audiences in 1969 saw **The Wild Bunch**, they reacted. Some were appalled, repelled. Some were galvanized, electrified. The sweaty close-ups, grungy anti-heroes and casual brutality of the spaghetti westerns was one thing – the extended massacres

15

which opened and closed Peckinpah's magnum opus was something else altogether.

There was nothing conventional about his approach to the western. His characters, for all that they are a motley collection of outlaws and

thieves, are motivated more by guilt than gold, propelled towards their bloody final acts as much by a compromised sense of honour as a need for vengeance. Peckinpah's films are about men: the interaction of men, their psychology. And the male psyche has always had a tendency towards violence.

But if subtext and character development were paramount to Peckinpah, just as challenging were the images he put on screen. From the first scene of children prodding scorpions into

Agonizing deaths in the closing scenes of *The Wild Bunch*

a swarming mass of red ants, to the ritualistic killing of a Mexican freedom fighter which provokes the climactic showdown none of the protagonists survive, Peckinpah's images of death are profound, sometimes poetic, always disturbing and never dishonest.

His main aesthetic achievement in the presentation of onscreen violence is the incorporation of slow-motion footage. Like Leone, he drew on Kurosawa for inspiration. In **The Seven Samurai** (1954), there is a poetry to the death scenes that belies the horror of the act: samurai duel with swords, an arcing blow is struck, both parties stand in absolute stillness for a horrible moment of uncertainty, then Kurosawa segues into slow-motion as one of them crumples, folding almost gracefully into himself as he hits the ground, a soft cloud of dust billowing from the impact.

Peckinpah took the technique further, shooting a scene from multiple angles at a variety of film speeds and then cross-cutting in order to isolate and protract the moment of death, retaining Kurosawa's visual poetry while still communicating the reality of violent demise. This is another parallel: the juxtaposition of mythic elements with grim realism. Codes of honour and issues of loyalty are expounded on in both *The Seven Samurai* and *The Wild Bunch*, while iconography emphasizes the characters' stature: the Bunch walking determinedly towards their destiny in Peckinpah's film; the samurai working as a disciplined fighting force, marshalling the villagers against their aggressors in Kurosawa's. Realism comes courtesy of the rain-soaked finale in *The Seven Samurai*, where the bandits are brought down from their horses and progressively decimated while the samurai themselves lose several of their number, and in the agonizing deaths so unflinchingly depicted in the closing scenes of *The Wild Bunch*.

Yet for all their aesthetic validity, for all that they further the tradition of a director as venerated as Kurosawa, Peckinpah's films are often reviled for their violent content and for what many see as a tendency to misogyny. (See the next chapter for a discussion of the representation of women in violent films.) Nonetheless, he remains a hugely influential figure. Of all the filmmakers who owe him a debt of gratitude – from Walter Hill to Robert Rodriguez – it is perhaps John Woo who has most successfully emulated Peckinpah's integration of dynamic visuals with character motivation based on honour, loyalty and friendship. Interestingly, this arc of influence – Kurosawa, Peckinpah, Woo – demonstrates a cultural demographic, from east to west to east[4].

A marauding bandit brought down in *The Seven Samurai*

Heroic bloodshed: the impact of the Hong Kong action movie

Hong Kong movies are among the most extreme examples of filmmaking. The emphasis is on action, usually to the detriment of narrative. The violence is graphic, be it by gun, sword, foot or fist. A sub-genre, Category III, adds explicit sexual content to the melange. The proceedings are often offset by swathes of broad comedy that border on farce. Many of these films can seem interminable despite the speed and ferocity of the fight scenes. The appeal – at least until the films of John Woo began to emerge in the late Eighties and early Nineties – was limited to a certain cult audience.

17

'Heroic bloodshed' is a term used to define a genre of Hong Kong cinema where the action is more likely to involve shoot-outs and car chases than extended bouts of kung fu, and where the milieu (usually the criminal underworld) is more instantly recognizable to western audiences. It is the genre in which Woo became famous. ***A Better Tomorrow*** (1986) was his first film to enjoy widespread distribution in the west. The influence of Peckinpah is evident in Woo's use of slow-motion, different film speeds and rapid intercutting; moreover, Peckinpah's prevalent theme of former friends or partners finding themselves allayed on opposite sides of the law is rendered even more poignantly in *A Better Tomorrow*. Here, it is brothers who come into conflict. Kit (Leslie Cheung) is an idealistic cop whose dedication to his job tips over into obsession; his elder sibling Ho (Ti Lung), assisted by his best friend Mark (Chow Yun Fat), profits from forged currency while keeping his criminal activities hidden from his family. However, when a deal goes bad, Ho is betrayed, his father assassinated, and Kit's career in the police force compromised. Released from prison, Ho tries to rebuild his relationship with Kit, help his friend Mark (who has been reduced to menial work for the new gang boss), and stay on the straight and narrow. But it's not long before he is drawn back into the criminal underworld.

The violence is graphic but highly stylized, notably in the scene where Mark stages a retributive hit against Ho's betrayer, who is dining with associates and bodyguards at an upmarket restaurant. Dressed in a sharp suit and a floor-length overcoat, slow-motion rendering him instantly iconic, Mark strides along a corridor towards the room the private party is occupying, stashing handguns behind the foliage of potted plants. Bursting in and executing his victim at point-blank range, Mark then retreats along the corridor, availing himself of the weaponry as the bodyguards pursue him, tossing each pistol away as he empties it.

Woo consolidated the success of *A Better Tomorrow* with ***The Killer*** (1989), an even more stylish and iconic action thriller. The dynamic is similar: the protagonists are cop and criminal, men of honour in a world of violence and betrayal. Unorthodox detective Lee (Danny Lee) tracks down philosophical hitman Jeff (Yun Fat), a man whose doubts over his profession have been exacerbated by his accidental blinding of nightclub singer Jenny (Sally Yeh) in a shoot-out. He agrees to a final job in order to finance an operation that will restore her sight, only to be targeted by his employer when his identity is revealed.

As relations become increasingly strained between Lee and his colleagues, so his affinity with Jeff develops. The stunning finale has them stand against Jeff's betrayers in an old church, flickering candles and white doves providing a counterpoint to the balletic gun battle; violence as visual poetry. Again, Woo's use of slow-motion and editing are exemplary: he is easily the most distinguished practitioner of these techniques since Peckinpah.

While never skimping on action, Woo's films go against the grain of most Hong Kong movies in that narrative and characterization are the impetus for the set-pieces; nor does he use slapstick to plug the gaps between shoot-outs. All of his characters pay for their use of violence.

Woo made an inauspicious move to Hollywood with the pedestrian Jean-Claude Van Damme vehicle *Hard Target* (1993) and the disappointing *Broken Arrow* (1996), before striking box office gold with *Face/Off* (1997) and *Mission: Impossible 2* (1999). Sadly, none of his American projects have matched the depth and emotional integrity of his Hong Kong work.

Empire magazine has described Woo as 'the undisputed master of high-octane cinema … the most copied filmmaker working today', citing, as well as Peckinpah, his influences as Martin Scorsese and Stanley Donen[5]. Add to that list Michael Cimino. On a thematic level, what is probably Woo's most violent film, the Vietnam-set **Bullet in the Head** (1990), comes across as an eastern *Deer Hunter*. Following the fortunes (and more often misfortunes) of a group of friends – Ben (Tony Leung), Frank (Jacky Cheung) and Paul (Waise Lee) – united, and later divided, by the pursuit of wealth, *Bullet in the Head* begins in the streets of Hong Kong. Violence is part of everyday life. There is rioting and social disaffection. Predatory street gangs are rife. Ben's wedding banquet is disturbed when Paul, who has borrowed money from a loan shark to finance his friend's big day, is set upon by gang leader Ringo and his thugs. Paul sustains a severe beating rather than hand over the money. Ben and Frank band together and stage a retributory attack, killing Ringo. The three friends flee to Saigon where they fall in with Luke (Simon Yam), a charismatic mercenary who is as willing to perform assassinations as he is to steal gold in his quest for financial betterment.

Unlearning all the lessons of unity and the negative effects of violence that their experiences in Hong Kong should have taught them, they embark upon a series of misadventures where robbery and wholesale massacre of anyone who stands in their way is the order of the day, their dark odyssey driving them deeper into war-torn

Vietnam. Finally, even the bonds of friendship disintegrate when Paul, obsessed with their shipment of stolen gold, provokes a Mexican stand-off with Ben and Frank. Events are curtailed when they are captured by the Viet Cong. In a stand-in for the Russian roulette sequence in Cimino's film, POWs are forced to shoot fellow prisoners for the amusement of the VC. Ben participates in order to affect their escape, a morally questionable decision but a matter of survival. Paul's behaviour is even more reprehensible. Fleeing the stronghold, he shoots Frank in the head when, injured, he presents a liability; then, in order to steal a boat, murders a group of unarmed villagers. The film ends back in Hong Kong with Paul, now a successful businessman, challenged by Ben over his act of treachery. Their fight to the death is as protracted and brutal as anything in Hong Kong cinema.

A militaristic re-imagining of 'heroic bloodshed' genre conventions is also evident in Samo Hung's *Eastern Condors* (1986), which freely borrows its plot from Robert Aldrich's *The Dirty Dozen* (1967). However, such 'borrowings' work both ways. Ringo Lam's *City on Fire* (1987), the tale of an undercover cop caught in a Mexican stand-off when a falling out among thieves escalates, provides the template for Quentin Tarantino's *Reservoir Dogs*; while Chow Yun Fat's two-handed gunplay in *A Better Tomorrow* is revisited by Harvey Keitel in Tarantino's film[6].

Hollywood had flirted with martial arts in the Seventies, cashing in on the popularity of Bruce Lee by staging kung-fu scenes in films like *The Yakuza* (Sydney Pollack, 1974) and *The Killer Elite* (Peckinpah, 1975). Thanks to Woo's box office clout, the trend has re-emerged, highly stylized sequences featuring prominently in *The Matrix* (Andy and Larry Wachowski, 1999), and making a box-office success of Ang Lee's mystical *Crouching Tiger, Hidden Dragon* (2001). At the time of writing, it has been announced that martial arts are to feature in Quentin Tarantino's forthcoming *Kill Bill*.

Defining the moment: the cinema of Quentin Tarantino

There is usually one filmmaker who defines a decade: arguably Scorsese for the Seventies; Spielberg for typifying the blockbuster ethos of the Eighties; the re-emergence of Steven Soderbergh so far this decade. There can be little dispute that the Nineties were the time of Tarantino. He came out of nowhere with *Reservoir Dogs* (1991). A slice of effortless cool, the film came complete with its own endlessly debatable enigma (who shot Nice Guy Eddie?), a soundtrack which married image and music as stylishly as anything by Scorsese, and a delicious non-sequitur of a title that brought to mind *Straw Dogs* (Peckinpah, 1971) and stirred up the old movie violence furore just as powerfully, particularly with its torture scene (see chapter two). It dripped with iconography – sharp black suits, cool shades – and every line of dialogue was hip and instantly quotable. It simultaneously revitalized the gangster genre and treated it with self-conscious irony. And it spawned a slew of imitators: *Things to Do in Denver When You're Dead* (Gary Fleder, 1995), *Two Days in the Valley* (John Herzfeld, 1996). Even *The Usual Suspects* (1995) and *Lock, Stock and Two Smoking Barrels* (1998), which established directors Bryan Singer and Guy Ritchie in their own right, owe a debt to Tarantino.

Famously, Tarantino started out working in a video rental store. He has said that the inspiration for *Reservoir Dogs* came from watching a different heist movie each day for a week. Indeed, one of the film's many noteworthy qualities is the iconoclastic manner in which its director leaves out the heist entirely, structuring it so that the planning and aftermath of the robbery are contrasted throughout.

That Tarantino's education in cinema was hands-on and populist, as opposed to being formally tutored at film school, is precisely the reason that his work is so immediate and full-blooded: he draws upon an avid movie buff's understanding and love of a hundred years of the art. Cine-literate is perhaps the term that describes him best. A scene in his second film, the blackly comic **Pulp Fiction** (1994), demonstrates perfectly his ability to utilize instantly recognizable visual references, keying his own narrative in to the audience's familiarity with other movies, while at the same time delivering these homages with a sense of ironic playfulness.

The scene in question has down-on-his-luck pugilist Butch (Bruce Willis) on the run from gang boss Marcellus Wallace (Ving Rhames), having not only won the fight he was supposed to throw, but also killed his opponent in the ring. A chance encounter and an attempted hit-and-run on Butch's part sees them both injured and bleeding as they blunder, still hell-bent on killing each other, into a pawn shop owned by Maynard (Duane Whitaker). Maynard separates them at gunpoint, then lays them out with the stock of his shotgun. Then, having tied them up in the cellar, calls his friend Zed (Peter Greene) and invites him over for an afternoon of homosexual rape.

21

They set about Marcellus first, while Butch is kept watch over by the Gimp, a demented creature dressed in bondage gear and kept on a leash. Butch frees himself from his bonds, punches the Gimp out and makes tracks. Halfway out of the shop, he hears Marcellus's muffled cries. Never mind their antagonism, Butch goes back for him. But before he does, he scours the pawn shop for a weapon. He considers the respective merits of a hammer (*The Toolbox Murders*), baseball bat (*The Untouchables*), chainsaw (*The Texas Chain Saw Massacre*) and – the implement he finally chooses – a samurai sword. This latter references a whole range of movies, from *The Seven Samurai* to bizarre cult favourite *Shogun Assassin* (Kenji Misumi, 1980). Here, Tarantino's love of movies is at its most open and non-judgemental, tipping a nod to the notable and the notorious, as well as sending up his own reputation as an enfant terrible of movie violence. Moreover, the scene makes a sly comment about the readiness of cinema to seize upon whatever is to hand for its moments of mayhem and murder.

Hardware: the weapon as icon

Writing of the films of Dario Argento, Maitland McDonagh notes the 'oneiric phallocentricity'[7] of knives, often the weapon of choice in horror/stalk-and-slash films. It's an apposite turn of phrase. The barrel of a gun or rocket launcher, the blade of a knife or sword, a baseball bat, a piece of lead piping – virtually every weapon one can think of is an inherently phallic symbol. Appropriate, since it's generally men who use these implements.

Feelin' lucky? Clint Eastwood in **Dirty Harry**

In **Dirty Harry** (Don Siegel, 1971), hard-nosed cop Harry Callaghan (Clint Eastwood) lives by the gun to such a degree that he soliloquizes about it when he gets the drop on a (still armed) criminal: 'I know what you're thinking, punk: *did he fire six shots or only five?* Well, to tell you the truth I've forgotten myself in all this excitement. But since this is a .44, *the* most powerful handgun in the world – could blow your head clean off – you've gotta ask yourself one question: *do I feel lucky?* Well, do you, punk?'

The combination of this dialogue, the stature of an actor like Eastwood, and the sheer size of the handgun in question, make the scene truly iconic. However, when the criminal surrenders his weapon rather than take the chance, sullenly adding 'I got to know' (i.e. whether Harry's gun was loaded or not), Callaghan pulls the trigger on an empty chamber. By the end of the film – having risked suspension for violation of a suspect's rights, and suffered a pistol-whipping in his pursuit of the sociopathic Scorpio Killer (Andrew Robinson) – he repeats the speech. This time his nemesis calls his bluff. Callaghan's gun roars and the tax-payers are spared the cost of a trial. The sexual metaphor is obvious: at the beginning of the film, Callaghan is impotent (out of ammunition); the Scorpio Killer presents further challenges to his machismo; Callaghan reasserts his masculinity by shooting him (ammunition = potency) at the denouement.

Gun-worship is a key factor of crime films, film noir and gangster epics (see chapter three). However, as the aforementioned scene in *Pulp Fiction* shows, many other forms of weaponry have proved popular, not least the unorthodox use of tools. In addition to the examples already cited, consider Abel Ferrera's *The Driller Killer* (1979), or the Coen brothers' Oscar-nominated *Fargo* (1996), where a luckless character is fed into a wood-chipping machine. *A Nightmare on Elm Street* (Wes Craven, 1984) takes the knife imagery so beloved of the stalk-and-slash genre a step further. Freddy Krueger (Robert Englund), the disfigured and demonic villain of the piece, isn't content just to use a knife; he sports a glove, each of the five fingers of which terminate in a sharp, tapering blade. As in *Dirty Harry*, weapon and user become fused in the popular consciousness.

James Cameron's **The Terminator** (1984), takes it further: Arnold Schwarzenegger's cyborg is not only the main character (the film, after all, takes its title from him), but also a weapon unto itself. He is, quite literally, a killing machine. The film opens with a vignette set in 2029: following a nuclear holocaust, machines have developed into self-operational beings intent on destroying mankind. The first shot shows a tank-like machine crunching over a pile of human skulls. The scene quickly shifts to the present, and again the milieu is introduced with a shot of a machine, this time a garbage truck. Flickers of lightning from a sudden electrical storm dart around the cab. There is a burst of white light and the Terminator appears, in the form of a man. Stark naked. It approaches a gang of street punks, intent on procuring a set of clothes. They ridicule it. It responds by dispatching them with efficiency and economy. Its next stop is a gun shop, where it arms itself with pistols, shotguns and an Uzi sub-machine gun. Rather than acquaint itself with cash transactions or credit card payments, it executes the store-keeper.

What follows is basically a chase movie with a simple plot. The machines have sent the Terminator back through time to kill Sarah Connor (Linda Hamilton), the mother of rebel leader John Connor, before she even becomes pregnant with him. Result: no threat to their supremacy. The rebels counter by sending freedom fighter Kyle Reese (Michael Biehn) after the Terminator – his mission: to protect Sarah. The violence is continual: the Terminator works by process of elimination, killing every woman in the city who shares Sarah's name. Finally tracking her to a nightclub, it wipes out swathes of innocent bystanders. When Sarah is taken into protective custody, it storms the police precinct, shotgun in one hand, Uzi in the other, casually decimating New York's finest. This scene, gratuitous as it is, is also hugely iconic: dressed in biker leathers, shades on, the Terminator unhurriedly stalks the corridors of the precinct, both guns blazing.

For two-thirds of the film, while the Terminator is in human guise, it demonstrates certain human aspects: it speaks, uses modes of communication (telephones) and transport (cars, bikes, trucks), and has recourse to weaponry. By the end of the film, as it pursues Sarah and Kyle into a foundry, its human exterior has been burned away to reveal skeletal chrome, lenses for eyes. It has reverted to pure machine, all human attributes lost: no longer does it attempt to communicate; no longer does it need guns. It has become its own weapon. With bitter irony, after human cunning and bravery have only gone so far in combating it, the Terminator is defeated only when Sarah utilizes a metal press: the machine is destroyed by a machine.

In **Duel** (Spielberg, 1972), the weapon all but replaces its user. The streamlined narrative, unencumbered by provenance or subplot, has sales rep David Mann (Dennis Weaver) run afoul of a big grimy old Mack truck on a stretch of deserted highway. The rep's name is an obvious clue to the film's aesthetic: man versus machine. The truck, first introduced in a low-angled shot that fills the frame with the radiator grille and makes it impossible to discern anything behind the windscreen, soon takes on its own ominous, looming, relentless

Man versus machine in Steven
Spielberg's *Duel*

personality. The driver, on the other hand, is a cipher. All that is seen
of him is an arm extended from the cab window, beckoning Mann
to overtake; a hand on the steering wheel as the truck pulls in behind
Mann at a gas station; a pair of cowboy boots glimpsed in the gap
between the ground and the chassis, kicking the tyres; a hand gripping
the gear lever as the truck rams Mann's car at the film's climax.

The driver's motives are equally shrouded. Mann's only vaguely
antagonistic act is to overtake him. Nor does the truck threaten
anyone else; it even stops to offer assistance to a school bus in need
of a push by the side of the road. And with the amount of doubling
back the truck does in order to further menace Mann, not to
mention waiting around blind curves for him, engine idling, the
driver doesn't seem bothered about delivering any load. The truck's
articulated trailer is a rusty tanker marked 'Flammable'. Yet when it
plunges over a cliff at the end, there is no explosion. Ergo, he's not
carrying anything.

Ultimately, the driver is only there because trucks can't drive
themselves. *Duel* is basically an existential thriller as fuelled by Mann's
mounting sense of paranoia as the Mack truck is by diesel. The truck,
snorting black smoke (another self-evident pointer, this time to the
'creature feature' B-movies of the Fifties), has simply singled him out,
and the film's 86-minute running time charts a steady escalation from
cat-and-mouse game to battle for survival. Man versus machine; and
Mann only wins when he sacrifices his own machine, his battered
and underpowered car, luring the truck to the edge of the cliff.

The art of cool

As we have seen, cinema is a self-reverential medium, particularly where iconography is concerned. There is the direct approach: the remake (*The Seven Samurai* relocated to the wild west as *The Magnificent Seven*); or the homage, which is more an acknowledgement of influence. Compare, for instance, the black-suited criminals in *Reservoir Dogs* with the characters essayed by Frank Sinatra, Dean Martin, et al. in the 'Rat Pack' movies of the Sixties[8]. The common denominator is the presentation of protagonists in iconic terms – colloquially, to make them look as cool as possible.

To this end, costume and composition have always been of utmost importance. The well-worn western garb of the surviving members of the outlaw band in *The Wild Bunch* is indicative of their rugged masculinity; the way the camera frames them is positively mythic. The biker leathers worn by Johnny (Marlon Brando) in **The Wild One** (Laslo Benedek, 1953) bespeak the character's moody anti-authoritarianism. Viewed fifty years on, the film seems tame, but it was banned in the UK until 1967. Iconography abounds as Johnny and his biker gang ride into a small town, 'looking for someone to shove 'em around so they can get sore and show how tough they are'. Apart from a brawl with a rival outfit led by the grungy but charismatic Chino (Lee Marvin), there is little actual harm done. Instead, it is the townspeople who have recourse to violence when ill feelings about the bikers and resentment over the sheriff's ineffectuality in running them out of town lead to vigilante tactics. A lynch mob forms and Johnny is given a beating. Later, trying to escape, a thrown tyre-iron knocks him off his bike. The machine, riderless, careens into a bystander, killing him, a fatality the townsfolk try to pin on Johnny.

A sense of woolly liberalism pervades the latter stages of the film (one wonders if its plea for understanding on behalf of its delinquent protagonist played a part in the banning), somewhat deflating it. Nonetheless, *The Wild One*'s visual style still impresses, as does Brando's sullen performance. In the film's most celebrated line, a girl in a coffee shop asks what he's rebelling against. 'Whaddya got?' he replies.

The Wild One and *The Wild Bunch* have more in common than the adjective in their titles: they are about refusal to conform, a powerful enough subject in itself. But more than that, they are about men who look cool even as they demonstrate this refusal. Thus creating the movie icon.

taking it to the limit

CHAPTER TWO

Every form of art has to challenge, provoke and push back its own boundaries, constantly questioning and redefining itself in order to survive. Cinema is no exception. Filmmakers of note have always striven to take things that bit further. Filmmakers who are artists do so not for sensationalism but to genuinely expand the possibilities of their chosen medium.

There are those for whom the image itself is the most immediate aspect of their work, who challenge the audience with visual non-sequiturs that are as surreal as they are memorable. Luis Buñuel, decades before his art-house triumphs *Belle de Jour* (1967) and *The Discreet Charm of the Bourgeoisie* (1972), teamed up with Salvador Dali to make the startling 17-minute short **Un Chien Andalou** (1928). It starts with an eyeball being sliced by a razor, a scene all the more shocking for having no narrative context – and it still shocks 75 years on. Yet the image is crucial. The eye is the primary tool by which we appreciate cinema: a shot of one being cut into forces us to do one of two things – look away, or look at things in a different light.

Milestones

In some ways *Un Chien Andalou* is typical of its era, when experimentalism in cinema (which was, essentially, the new kid on the block as far as forms of artistic expression were concerned) was yet to be tempered by the constraints of commercialism. Things changed in 1930 with the introduction of the Hayes Code. Granted, this was an American phenomenon, but since America has always been the biggest market for movies, the knock-on effect as regards the distribution of British and European films was not inconsiderable. The Hayes Code basically sanitized, to an almost puritanical degree, what the discerning adult was permitted to see onscreen. Violence – indeed, any form of visceral imagery – perforce became implicit as opposed to explicit. Romantic scenes were akin to a game of snooker: one or both feet had to remain on the ground. Even the length of time two characters were permitted to kiss was regulated.

It was this ludicrous form of bowdlerization that Alfred Hitchcock kicked against in *Notorious* (1946): by having his romantic leads (Cary Grant and Ingrid Bergman) smooch during a long-distance telephone call that Grant is trying to make, Hitchcock was able to intersperse their moments of intimacy with enough dialogue (albeit fragmentary) to sneak the scene past the censors.

Fourteen years later, and still constrained as to what he could put on screen, Hitchcock made his most brilliantly constructed and suspensefully sustained attack on the boundaries of mainstream cinema. ***Psycho*** (1960) fixates on sexuality (the first scene has Marion Crane [Janet Leigh] lounging on a motel room bed in bra and slip having just indulged in some lunch-hour licentiousness) and twisted psychology (nominal villain of the piece Norman Bates [Anthony Perkins] is a mother-obsessed, cross-dressing sociopath). It also defies audience expectations as a matter of course. Marion is set up as the heroine, albeit a flawed one (she goes on the lam after ripping off her boss); the first half hour details her flight and almost-arrest. So far, only the title is any indication that what is to follow is anything other than a low-key, character-driven crime thriller.

Unforgettable imagery in Hitchcock's *Psycho*

But then – after a very unwise choice of stopovers – Marion's centrality to the film is swiftly and shockingly curtailed in one of cinema's most celebrated and unforgettable scenes. In this – the shower scene – Hitchcock delivers his masterstroke. Bearing in mind that the key elements to this scene are nudity (emphasizing Marion's vulnerability at this point, as well as casting the audience as voyeurs and therefore complicit) and violent death (not only is the knife phallic, but the blood swirling down the plughole is very Freudian in terms of metaphor[1]), the potential for public outrage and the film's revilement was huge. *Psycho* was released, it must be remembered, only a year after the controversy over *Peeping Tom* (see chapter five) did irreparable damage to Michael Powell's career. It could have been Hitchcock's undoing.

But the maestro judged his approach perfectly. The shower scene – while as intense, emotive and jolting as anything in cinema (made doubly effective by Bernard Herrmann's score) – is a masterpiece of the suggestive over the explicit. Apart from a very brief, and slightly unfocused, overhead shot of Marion, hands covering her body, there is no nudity on display: it is all head-and-shoulders or below-the-knee. The editing creates a montage of images – the silhouetted killer, the knife being raised or plunged down (it is never actually seen to strike), Marion's hand clutching the shower rail, the swirl of blood as it is washed away by the still-spurting shower – which, collectively, leave the audience thinking they have seen more than they really have.

Twelve years later, Hitchcock was making ample use of a less censorious aesthetic. ***Frenzy*** (1973) begins with the sighting, by a crowd of Londoners, of a naked female body washed up on the banks of the Thames. What follows is a thinly plotted tale of the wrong man, Richard Blaney (Jon Finch), an ex-RAF officer with a history of domestic violence, suspected of a series of sexual murders. Financial embarrassments and a sacking from a dead-end job behind the bar of a seedy pub engender a spate of ill-tempered incidents, which are taken as evidence against him when his ex-wife Brenda (Barbara Leigh-Hunt) becomes the killer's latest victim.

The perpetrator, in a rather self-evident bit of irony, is Blaney's only friend, Robert Rusk (Barry Foster). The film plays out in counterpoint, Blaney finding himself increasingly in the frame as Rusk covers his tracks. The sexual violence is shocking even by *Psycho*'s standards. Whereas the nastiness at the Bates Motel is mostly suggestive, *Frenzy* is direct to the point of misogyny. Not only is the dialogue rife with juvenile sexual references, but also Brenda's rape and strangulation are shown in protracted and graphic detail.

The dehumanization of the act is revisited in the film's major set-piece when Rusk, having hoisted his next victim's corpse into the back of a lorry (a more subtle ironic touch here, since Rusk is every inch the spiv, his business the redistribution of things that have, to use the old adage, fallen off the back of a lorry), realizes he has left behind a vital bit of evidence. Compelled to go back, he is struggling to retrieve the item, an ornamental lapel-pin, when the truck moves off. The pin is clasped between the corpse's fingers, now stiff with rigor mortis. Rusk, obliged to lie prostrate so as not to reveal his presence among the sacks of potatoes that comprise the truck's load, splays the corpse's legs apart, rolling on top of it in a grotesque parody of rape, then proceeds to break the fingers to get at the lapel pin.

The rape scene is ugly; this necrophiliac re-enactment of it even more so. It demonstrates the degree of onscreen excess not available to Hitchcock just over a decade previously, as well as indicating that, the freer he was to show the explicit, the less panache he displayed as a filmmaker.

It took John Boorman's **_Deliverance_** (1972) to push back the envelope of sexual violence to include a mainstream depiction of homosexual rape. Adapted from James Dickey's novel, the film begins with four friends – Ed (Jon Voight), Lewis (Burt Reynolds), Bobby (Ned Beatty) and Drew (Ronny Cox), white-collar city-dwellers all – embarking on a canoeing trip. Their intent is to make their way down 'the last wild, untamed, unpolluted, unfucked-up river in the south' before it is dammed and the landscape is changed forever. A noble sentiment. However, their idealism is soon put to the test when they discover that it's not just the river that's wild and untamed.

Pulling in to the bank, Ed and Bobby are waylaid by a pair of hillbillies, who hold them at gunpoint. Ed is tied to a tree, a strap tightened around his neck, and tortured with a knife. Worse is the indignity suffered by Bobby. Forced to strip, he is brutalized by one of the hillbillies, made to 'squeal like a piggie', and anally raped.

Lewis, the only member of the foursome equipped with some form of weapon (a crossbow), manages to intervene before a similar fate can befall Ed. He shoots one of the hillbillies; the other flees. The scene comes at less than halfway through the film, and the ensuing debate on the moral and legal consequences of the situation lifts it above the conventions of the thriller genre. And although the foursome face further tribulations – Drew is killed shooting white-water rapids, Lewis is injured, Ed is forced to abandon his liberal beliefs and go up against the surviving hillbilly who still threatens them – _Deliverance_ develops less as an adventure film than an examination of how 'civilized' behaviour disintegrates when the normal social mores cease to apply. The conclusion has nothing to do with macho heroics, but charts their reliance on lies, deceit and a conspiracy of silence when they arrive at a township at the end of their river trip and are called upon to account for their misadventures.

Nonetheless, it is the 'squeal like a piggie' scene that remains the most potent and disturbing moment in the film, a predecessor of equally graphic scenes of sexual assault by men against men in _Scum_ (Alan Clarke, 1979) and _Pulp Fiction_.

Sexual violence has proved one of the more uneasy aspects of cinema, particularly from the Seventies onwards. Violence against women (discussed in detail elsewhere in this chapter) stretches back to the likes of **The Public Enemy** (William Wellman, 1931), where gangster Tom Powers (James Cagney) responds to the breakfast table haranguing of his moll (Mae Clarke) by ramming a grapefruit into her face. This might seem like small change compared to *Psycho*'s shower scene or Brenda's ignominious demise in *Frenzy*, but in the context of Powers' progression from small-time bootlegger to remorseless killer, it affirms his credentials as a man who cares about nothing. (The scene is worth comparing with Michael Corleone's mistreatment of his wife in *The Godfather* and *The Godfather Part II* – see chapter three.)

An interesting counterpoint to violence in gangster movies, where wives and molls are equally as likely to be on the receiving end of a mobster's brutality as a rival gang member or an authority figure, is the similar milieu explored in Martin Scorsese's **Raging Bull** (1980) – a milieu of bars and tenements where the lives and conflicts of working-class Italian-Americans are played out. It is from this background that Jake La Motta (Robert de Niro) struggles to rise, not through criminal enterprise but just as bloodily – with his fists, in the ring. Which is not to say that his endeavours are not shadowed by the criminal underworld, in the shape of dodgy boxing promoters and the wise-guy neighbourhood types his brother Joey (Joe Pesci) is associated with. Joey's lot in life is not particularly enviable, either: treated offhandedly by Jake for no other reason than being the younger sibling, he takes upon himself the equally thankless role of La Motta's manager. La Motta's violent temperament is not just confined to the ring, and Joey finds his loyalties tested as his brother's life spins out of control.

Taking his punishment in the ring: Robert de Niro as Jake LaMotta in *Raging Bull*

La Motta convinces himself that his wife Vickie (Cathy Moriarty) is seeing other men, fixating on neighbourhood smooth-talker Salvy (Frank Vincent). Joey takes matters into his own hands, attacking Salvy in a nightclub. The fight spills outside, Joey incapacitating Salvy and, while he is unable to protect himself, slamming a car door against his head. The incident does nothing to ameliorate Jake's imagined jealousies, and he soon accuses Joey of having an affair with Vickie himself. Despite their protestations, he resorts to violence against both of them.

Raging Bull devotes considerably more of its running time to documenting La Motta's tendency to domestic violence than to the legitimized violence he committed in the ring. Nonetheless, the boxing scenes are as gruelling as anything that has been put on screen. For it is in the ring that La Motta takes his punishment for the wrongs he has done and the pain he has caused in his personal relationships. The 1956 fight with 'Sugar' Ray Robinson (Johnny Barnes) follows his maltreatment of his wife and his brother. Pinned against the ropes, he offers no defence, taking blow after blow. Michael Chapman's exemplary black-and-white cinematography captures the gouts of blood and sweat that erupt from La Motta's face with every impact of Robinson's glove.

Finally, abandoned by Joey, estranged from Vickie, La Motta is arrested for soliciting minors at the nightclub he owns. Unable to raise bail, he is incarcerated. Locked in a cell alone, he is left with no opponent but himself. Howling with inexpressible rage, he pounds his fists into the wall, hammering at his own shadow.

Raging Bull, in its final scenes, internalizes its protagonist's violence. Decades earlier, Tod Browning's **Freaks** (1932) incited controversy, so much so that it was banned in the UK for 30 years, by externalizing its visceral elements. Superficially, it's a lurid melodrama set in a travelling circus. Trapeze artist Cleopatra (Olga Baclanova) and strongman Hercules (Henry Victor) are the only two physically normal members of the retinue, and as much for this reason as any other they become lovers. The others are all sideshow freaks: some are midgets, some are hideously deformed; there is even a human torso. The narrative centres around Hans (Harry Earles), a midget who is smitten with Cleopatra. Beautiful but cruel and avaricious, she initially mocks him. On learning that he has an inherited fortune, however, she swiftly becomes responsive to his advances.

Hans's friends, the seal-trainer Venus (Leila Hyams) and Phroso the clown (Wallace Ford), try to warn him off, but he is too obsessed with Cleopatra to heed them. Cleopatra and Hercules devise a plot: Cleopatra will agree to marry Hans, they will then poison him – slowly so that his death will seem the result of a protracted, debilitating illness – and abscond with his money. At the wedding, the freaks encircle Cleopatra, joining in a chant of, 'We accept you. One of us.' She and Hercules mock them.

Over the coming weeks, the plot to kill Hans is put into motion. Realizing that something is amiss, the freaks come to his aid. Meanwhile, Hercules grows frustrated that while Cleopatra is acting the part of Hans's wife he cannot consummate his passion for her. He looks elsewhere, fixing his sights on Venus, whom he tries to rape. As he subdues her, Phroso intervenes, attacking him with a knife. Hercules, wounded, tries to find shelter in a nearby forest. It is night; a heavy rain falls. As Hercules, on his last legs, stumbles onwards, the freaks pursue him relentlessly. The human torso drags himself through the mud, a knife clamped between his teeth. Hercules dealt with, they return to settle the score with Cleopatra. As they close in around her, the chant goes up again: 'One of us … one of us … one of us.'

Freaks is a short film of slightly over an hour with a plot as slender as its running time. What makes it truly startling – and as great a challenge to onscreen propriety now as it must have seemed to audiences of its day – is Browning's use of real freaks. At one and the same time a work of demented genius and the most grotesque exploitation picture ever made, *Freaks* is a film whose horrors are absolutely real. Simulated scenes of violence or sex are one thing, but Browning's film makes a *raison d'être* of actual genetic deformity. The only make-up effect comes at the very end: the last shot is of Cleopatra, legs severed, hands deformed, face cut to ribbons, displayed at the circus's next venue, the most horrifying of exhibits.

Violence as ritual

Just as 'Ride of the Valkyries' is synonymous with *Apocalypse Now*, or 'Also Sprach Zarathustra' with *2001: A Space Odyssey*, 'Stuck in the Middle With You' by Steeler's Wheel will forever be associated with **Reservoir Dogs** (Tarantino, 1991). As with Coppola and Kubrick's movies, it's not just a piece of music on the soundtrack. It becomes part of the spatial fabric of the film, psychotic anti-hero Mr Blonde (Michael Madsen) performing a little dance to the song as he moves towards Marvin Nash (Kirk Baltz), the cop he is holding hostage, straight-razor in his hand.

No-one has been left in any doubt as to what is going down here; Blonde's boogie is prefaced with the laudably honest, if morally questionable homily, 'I'm not going to bullshit you … I don't really give a good fuck what you know or don't know, but I'm going to torture you anyway.' Yet when the music kicks in and Blonde

Michael Madsen as the sadistic
Mr Blonde in *Reservoir Dogs*

performs his soft-shoe shuffle, the effect is to draw the audience in –
then confront them with something ineffably nasty. Notwithstanding
that the bit of ear-slicing which follows is never actually seen (the
camera pans away, holding on the warehouse wall as Marvin's
screams, muffled by the electrical tape he has been gagged with,
supersede the music), it's an excruciating moment. But then again,
we're talking about torture – the deliberate and calculated infliction
of violence upon the defenceless by the barbarous – an act that can
hardly be depicted in a 'nice' way.

Those who denigrated *Reservoir Dogs* for its violent content (if
anything, the film's atmosphere is heavier with the threat of violence
than with actual violence) cited this scene above any other, proof that
what the human mind can conjure from a few visual prompts[2] is just
as disturbing as the darkest excesses of any artist in any medium.

The ritualistic elements of the torture scene – domination/
capitulation, restraint/bondage – have of themselves a darkly sexual
edge, which, as much as the actual violence, makes them troubling to
watch. Of perhaps even more concern are those scenes where the
ritual ends in death – be it execution or sacrifice. ***The Wicker
Man*** (Robin Hardy, 1973) begins with a staunchly Christian
policeman, Sergeant Howie (Edward Woodward), travelling alone
from the mainland to a small Scottish island, Summerisle, to
investigate the disappearance of a young girl.

Summerisle is a pagan community. Howie is so devout that he is
maintaining a celibate lifestyle until his marriage. It is for this reason

– his virginity – that he has been lured to the island. Increasingly at odds with Lord Summerisle (Christopher Lee), a liberated sensualist, Howie's fate is sealed in what ranks alongside *Seven* as one of the most devastating denouements ever filmed. Duped into attending, of his own volition, a place of sacrifice, he is forcibly restrained while schoolteacher Miss Rose (Diane Cilento), dressed in the robes of high priestess, informs him of his fate:

> **Miss Rose:** You will undergo death and rebirth. Resurrection, if you like. The rebirth, sadly, will not be yours but that of our crops.
> **Howie:** I am a Christian, and as a Christian I hope for resurrection. And even if you kill me now, it is I who will live again, not your damned apples.

This contrast between two belief systems, one orthodox, one rooted in supposedly less enlightened times, is carried through to the very last frame of the film. Howie is stripped, anointed, then dressed in a white robe, his arms held out at shoulder height in a crucifixion pose. The ritual is almost Christian in its iconography. But it takes a darker turn when he is hauled, hands tied, up a high promontory overlooking the sea. Here stands the wicker man. A huge grotesque effigy, ten times higher than a man, its base piled with kindling. Four men, holding torches, stand at the points of the compass around it. Howie realizes what is to happen; his cries of 'Oh God! Oh Jesus Christ! Oh my God! Christ!' are as much a reaction of panic as a reaffirmation of what he believes in.

A place of sacrifice: the pagan effigy in *The Wicker Man*

Cages built into the arms and upper torso of the wicker man house chickens and a goat. A door-like structure in the lower torso stands open, a ladder leading up to it. The subdued Howie, carried by a burly islander, is borne into the wicker man, and the door secured. Lord Summerisle leads his people in a prayer for bountiful crops. It is here that Howie conquers his fear and responds in kind.

Lord Summerisle: Mighty God of the Sun, bounteous Goddess of the Orchard, accept our sacrifice and make our blossoms fruit.
Islanders: Mighty God of the Sun, bounteous Godness …
Howie: Hear ye the words of the Lord. Awake, ye heathens. Behold, it is the Lord who has destroyed your crops for the truth has withered away.
Lord Summerisle: Reverence the sacrifice.

The effigy is set alight. The islanders sing as they perform a pagan dance around the conflagration. As the flames rise higher, Howie's behaviour again matches theirs, his voice ringing out in a rendition of the twenty-third psalm ('the Lord's my shepherd, I'll not want'). As the flames consume him, his final words are a plea to God not to be forgotten. The head of the wicker man collapses in on itself, a blood-red sunset taking the island as the effigy crumbles.

If the human sacrifice/fertility theme of *The Wicker Man* is a disturbing portrayal of paganism, then no less unsettling is the way that **Witchfinder General** (Michael Reeves, 1968) draws parallels between religious (again, Christian) fanaticism, ritual violence and sexual repression. Interestingly, its antagonists are both, ostensibly, men of faith. Richard (Ian Ogilvy) is a soldier trying to reconcile the violent reality of his duty to the crown (the film is played out against the backdrop of the English Civil War) with his puritanical faith in God. These diametric aspects of his personality sit side by side in a scene where he discovers that his fiancée Sara (Hilary Dwyer), a vicar's niece, has been attacked and raped. Instead of offering comfort, he insists that they pray together, then asks God's blessing upon the sword he swears vengeance with.

Richard's antagonist, whose henchmen are responsible for the atrocities against Sara, is Matthew Hopkins (Vincent Price), a self-appointed witchfinder. Hopkins is given to referring to himself as a lawyer. In its depiction of the law as a form of free enterprise in lawless times, not to mention its critical attitude towards the church and the army[3], *Witchfinder General* easily takes to task as many British institutions as Lindsay Anderson's *If…* (see chapter five).

The film starts with the image of a priest reading from the Bible as a young woman is hanged. It is suggested that a travesty has been made of the trappings of religion. This notion is reinforced when Sara's uncle is accused of being in league with the Devil, taken from his own church (a complete inversion of the persecuted being able to seek sanctuary therein), imprisoned and tortured. In order to prevent his summary execution, Sara agrees to provide sexual favours to Hopkins.

Every example of Hopkins's cruelty is played out in the shadow of the church, and has about it the iconography of religion: a woman accused of witchcraft is tied to a wooden upright (an obvious parallel with crucifixion) which is then lowered into a large bonfire; Hopkins threatens Sara with a brand in the shape of a crucifix. In conversation, Hopkins refers to his work as 'God's business'.

Hopkins's religious beliefs are revealed as a sham throughout the film; Richard's are questionable. At the climax, he and Sara are being held by Hopkins. The witchfinder tortures her in an attempt to elicit a confession of satanism from Richard. Richard remains mute as his fiancée screams, not taking his eyes from the scene; it is almost as if he is feeding his hate. Before Hopkins can have recourse to the brand, Richard's comrades-in-arms intervene. Freed, Richard takes an axe to Hopkins, striking him again and again. Horrified, one of the soldiers shoots Hopkins, finishing it. Richard rounds on the man, shrieking, 'You took him from me! You took him from me!' as Sara's screams redouble.

The ritualism of state-sanctioned (i.e. legal) executions is the basis of **The Green Mile** (1999), Frank Darabont's adaptation of Stephen King's novel. An early scene has the death row guards co-opt a trustee, an old prisoner who has earned certain privileges, as a 'stand-in' for the condemned man while they conduct a rehearsal for the execution. This extends to strapping him into the electric chair, clamps and electrodes in place, and miming the application of water to his head ('directs electricity straight to the brain, like a bullet') and the throwing of the switch.

With one exception – the sadistic Percy Whetmore (Doug Hutchinson) – the guards have no complicity in the executions they preside at. They are simply men doing their job. The film is set in the Depression: work is scarce and their jobs are something the guards perforce must hold down, never mind the more macabre aspects. It is through the threat of unemployment that Whetmore is able to exploit his connections (his uncle holds a gubernatorial position) in order to serve on the execution detail. Emotionally retarded, adolescent in his worldview, he is obsessed with not only witnessing death first hand, but also being a part of it. Reluctantly, warden Paul Edgecombe (Tom Hanks) puts him 'out front' (i.e. in charge of securing the prisoner to the chair and placing on his head the damp sponge) when the ritual is replayed, this time for real.

Despised by his colleagues, mocked by the death row inmates – in particular the condemned Eduard Delacroix (Michael Jeter) – Whetmore takes matters into his own hands when he applies the sponge to the Delacroix's head without first soaking it in water. The results are grotesque. Delacroix spasms, straining against his bonds as first one then another charge of electricity is passed through his body. Realizing what has happened, yet unable to do anything but see it through until Delacroix is dead, Edgecombe is forced to keep giving the instruction for the switch to be thrown. Delacroix takes a long time to die. His screams are agonizing. Behind the black hood pulled down over his head, his face burns.

As stated, Edgecombe and his other colleagues are only parts of the machinery of state executions. Whetmore is the renegade who exacerbates an already macabre process into a veritable carnival of horrors. The guilt of complicity here belongs to Whetmore, but King and Darabont use his actions to debate something bigger: the morality of ever taking a life, even if it is in payment for a life already taken.

Representation

Cinema's twin controversies have always been sex and violence. The promise of the erotic is often at the heart of character motivations, propelling heroes and villains alike towards acts of violence. This is practically the *raison d'être* of film noir: see chapter three. But there is a darker strand of cinema, where the sexual element of violence is inherent (and explicit) in the infliction of it. Paradoxically (or maybe not, since such scenes divide audiences and critics equally), the most extreme examples come from opposite ends of the filmic spectrum: art-house and exploitation.

From *Hiroshima, Mon Amour* (Alain Resnais, 1959) to *Intimacy* (Patrice Chéreau, 2001), art-house films have courted controversy with their frank approach to sexual expression. Fuelling the 'art or pornography' debate further were the likes of *I Am Curious – Yellow* (Vilgot Sjöman, 1967) and *Last Tango in Paris* (Bernado Bertolucci, 1972). But even *Last Tango*'s infamous butter scene seems coy compared to the degree of psycho-sexual obsession and violent consummation on display in Nagisa Oshima's **Ai No Corrida** (1976). The title translates as 'In the Realm of the Senses', which sounds romantic, sensual, but its *mise-en-scène* is far from it. The film begins with former prostitute Sada (Eiko Matsuda) seeking more legitimate work at a hostelry owned by Kichizo (Tatsuya Fuji). The seaminess of her erstwhile trade has not, however, left her with any disinclination towards sex. Far from it. She and Kichizo are soon embroiled in an affair, which functions purely on a level of physical gratification. Kichizo abandons his wife and his business. He and Sada relocate to a geisha house where, short of money, Sada returns to prostitution. Their sexual behaviour becomes ever more desperate and perverse. When even auto-eroticism fails to satiate them, Sada takes a knife (the phallic connotation hardly needs to be stated) and severs Kichizo's penis.

As troublesome and psychologically challenging as films about the violence of sex can be, less palatable are films dealing with violence against women. Generally speaking, these fall into two categories, both usually involving rape, and neither leaving the viewer feeling unsullied. There are films like *Death Wish* (Michael Winner, 1974), which uses an attack on the protagonist's wife as motivation for vigilante action. In other words, the woman suffers; the man achieves catharsis (see chapter three).

Then there is the equally seedy rape/revenge genre, where the woman's eventual triumph, and the punishment/demise of her male aggressors, are offered almost by way of excuse for earlier (usually protracted) scenes of rape, brutality and humiliation. Arguably the most extreme entry in this cycle is the infamous 'video nasty' (see chapter four for an analysis of this phenomenon) ***I Spit on Your Grave*** (Meir Zarchi, 1978). Its original title, *The Rape and Revenge of Jennifer Hill*[4], gives some indication of content, albeit perhaps understating things. Repeated rape is closer to the truth. Without dwelling too long on the synopsis, the eponymous would-be novelist (Camille Keaton[5]) leaves her city apartment for an isolated cabin in the country in order to work on her manuscript. Once there, she is targeted by a group of rednecks, one of whom is retarded (the suggestion is that they are the product of inbreeding). During a sickeningly protracted sequence that occupies almost the entire first half of the film, Jennifer is subjected to three gang rapes, one involving an act of sodomy with a beer bottle. Her cabin is laid to waste and her manuscript destroyed. The rest of the film is given over to her revenge. The rapists are variously hanged, castrated with a straight razor, bludgeoned with an axe and eviscerated by a speedboat's propeller.

The castration is, outside of the rape scenes, the most repellent aspect of the film. As an act of revenge, it occupies its proper place narratively, as well as being indicative of a punishment that fits the crime: sexual violation repaid by sexual violation. The way the scene is set up, however, is reprehensible: Jennifer has one of the rapists, Johnny, at gunpoint; she allows him to plead for his life, lowers her gun, then accompanies him into her cabin. There, they share a bath. She reaches for a concealed razor. Okay, there can be no doubt that Johnny suffers precisely the fate he deserves. But that doesn't alter the fact that the scene essentially depicts a rape victim seducing one of her tormentors.

In trading on the exultation of its latter scenes, allowing the audience to revel in acts of vengeance, no matter how graphic, *I Spit on Your Grave* seeks to ameliorate our unease at the earlier depiction of the woman as victim. The subtext – that the trauma of violence (worse, sexual violence) is negated by the shooting, bludgeoning, castration or otherwise of the perpetrator – is nauseating. The film makes no attempt to address the reality: that while external wounds heal, some internal ones never do.

Most films that feature scenes of rape – from Robert M Young's grubby exploitationer *Extremities* (1986) to Peter Greenaway's reviled art-house opus *The Baby of Mâcon* (1993) – do so without regard to the psychological implications of the act, or to its aftermath.

Peckinpah's **Straw Dogs** (1971) treats its subject with more gravity than most films of its ilk, containing a scene that, while significantly less protracted than *I Spit on Your Grave*, doesn't let the audience off easily. Moreover, it never loses sight of its victimized heroine Amy (Susan George) as the emotional centre of the film, her trauma effectively contrasted with the dehumanization (through use of violence) of first her tormentors, and then her husband David (Dustin Hoffman). Laden with a notorious reputation by dint of a video ban that has only recently been repealed (it has as little in common with the average 'video nasty' title as a Rembrandt has with a heavy metal album cover), it should also be noted that Peckinpah also deals with the aftermath, and deals with it seriously. Amy's fear and trauma are the focal points of the rape scene itself (her aggressors are depicted as being nothing other than brutal and animalistic), emotions that carry over into a subsequent sequence where David and Amy attend a church social. David has no idea of the attack his wife has been subject to (he sees out the remainder of the film in complete ignorance), and while he is coolly amused by a magic show staged for the village children, Amy goes through hell under the leering gazes of the men who violated her.

David's non-awareness of Amy's rape infuses the film's denouement with an even more critical view of the use of violence. When he turns on his attackers, it is not out of revenge for his wife, but because they have dared threaten the sanctity of his home. 'I will not permit violence against this house,' he declares, and loses no time in using excessive amounts of it himself. Utilizing gun, poker, and even a man trap, David dispatches his antagonists with clinical proficiency. Unusually among Peckinpah's protagonists, he survives to the end credits, but it is clear that his humanity is dead.

It is inarguable that the rape scene in *Straw Dogs* is disturbing (albeit disturbing for valid reasons), but what do we make of films where, although no explicit act of rape is shown, the concepts of sexuality and violence are so interlinked as to be undifferentiated? Where, in short, violent acts of sexual behaviour are not only responded to but also welcomed? **Duel in the Sun** (King Vidor, 1946) is one of the most perverse Hollywood productions of its era. Set against a series of melodramatic set pieces detailing the escalation of a land war, essentially it tells the story of two brothers divided by their affections for seductive 'half-breed' dancer Pearl Chavez (Jennifer Jones). Pearl's ferality is demonstrated unsubtly in a scene where she drinks from a mountain stream side-by-side with her horse (i.e. she's untamed). The brothers who fight and die over her are as much diametric opposites as they are clichés. Jesse McCanles (Joseph Cotten) is kind, considerate, sensitive and likeable. Lewt (Gregory Peck) is cruel, ruthless and given brutally to taking what he wants.

Guess which one she falls for?

During the course of a narrative which becomes more lurid with each scene, Lewt kills one of Pearl's early suitors, forces himself upon her, and finally kills his own brother when he develops a relationship with her. The consummation between Pearl and Lewt is a nastily ambiguous piece of film. Unlike, say, *Straw Dogs*, where every close-up of Amy shows her terrorized and traumatized by her ordeal, *Duel in the Sun* presents a scene that begins with Pearl cowering from Lewt's leering approach, only for her to react responsively at the crucial moment.

More graphic is the finale, which clearly links sex and death. Learning of Jesse's murder at his brother's hands, Pearl lures Lewt into the mountains, where she opens fire with a rifle, wounding him.

Immediately she starts crying. When Lewt wildly returns fire, she leaves off her wailing long enough to reload and emerge from her vantage point to finish him off. He shoots her twice, then starts crawling across the rockface, calling her name. For interminable minutes, they haul themselves painfully towards each other, calling out alternating pronouncements of love and hate. Bullet-ridden and bloody, they fall into each other's arms; they kiss, then die.

Duel in the Sun is deliberately referenced in Pedro Almodovar's **Matador** (1988). Equally lurid, but directed with a higher regard for irony, the film is a startling mixture of dark sexuality and camp farce. Almodovar starts as he means to go on: the opening credits sequence has bullfighting instructor Diego Montes (Nacho Martinez), a man who is as morbid as he is Priapic, indulging in a little self-abuse as he watches a series of clips from such 'video nasties' as *Bay of Blood* and *Bloody Moon* (see chapter four). Later, in a scene that really shouldn't be funny, his protégé Angel (Antonio Banderas), a repressed homosexual burdened by religious guilt and a mother complex, forces himself on Diego's girlfriend; his attempts to menace her with a knife become farcical when he opts to use a Swiss army knife and fumbles through every attachment until he finds the blade.

Angel's sense of guilt leads him to confess to a series of murders of which he is innocent. His defence counsel, Maria Cardenal (Assumpta Serna), realizes this when she discovers he is haemophobic. She, on the other hand, is excited by blood and death and, despite her profession, is not above killing for pleasure. This is evidenced in a scene where she lures a young stud to her room, seduces him and, at the point of orgasm, drives into the base of his neck a tapering blade hidden in her hairpin.

Maria soon comes into contact with Diego, whom she recognizes as a kindred spirit; needless to say, it is he who is responsible for the crimes Angel has confessed to. They chose the day of an eclipse to consummate their death-fixated passion. The prelude is absurdly romantic − a flickering log fire, a matador's cape strewn with rose petals spread before it. What follows is consummation as valediction; sex as a suicide pact.

Character motivations in *Matador* are psychologically more complex than in *Duel in the Sun*. The theme of sexual obsession is taken to its logical extreme when Diego and Maria die together in the throes of passion. She stabs him in the neck, then shoots herself. Their deaths are consensual, both in search of the ultimate orgasm. Notwithstanding Almodovar's artistic credentials as a filmmaker, however, the question still remains – as it does with any movie that features explicit sexual imagery – as to whether so graphic a depiction of the act is ever necessary, or simply an instrument used to provoke audience reaction, usually discomfort, which instantly renders such scenes memorable for having had that effect. *Matador's* denouement engenders a very potent sense of discomfort in its audience: when Diego and Maria take their need for gratification to lethal and irreversible lengths, it is a reminder that sex can function as a form of violence unto itself.

A taboo too far?

Sexual violence will always be controversial, but there is still one subject even more taboo: the placement/behaviour of children in situations where the darkest aspects of adulthood are suddenly made to apply. John Carpenter's **Halloween** (1978) begins with an extended point-of-view shot from the killer's perspective, roaming around the outside of a house where a teenage girl is entertaining her boyfriend. It's not long before they go upstairs and get serious[6]. The act completed, the boyfriend takes his leave with a vague promise to call her and the killer enters the house. Through the eyeholes of a mask, the camera scopes the interior as the killer mounts the stairs. The girl's bedroom door is pushed open; naked to the waist, she is brushing her hair in front of a mirror. Turning, she seems to recognize her stalker. Before she can protest, a knife appears. The girl is mercilessly butchered. It is only as the killer emerges from the house still clutching the bloodied knife that the perspective shifts, the subjective point of view is dispensed with, and his identity is revealed. An already unsettling scene – voyeurism, home invasion, the audience's enforced sense of complicity in the act – is taken into grimmer territory. The perpetrator is a prepubescent child dressed in a Halloween costume and outsized mask, the knife seeming all the bigger for the tiny hand it is clasped in.

Kinji Fukasaku's **Battle Royale** (2001) goes even further, depicting a totalitarian society where schoolchildren are compelled to fight each other to the death. The setting is millennial Japan; crime rates and truancy figures are at an unprecedented level. Delinquency is unchecked; teachers are knifed in school corridors. The government responds with the BR (Battle Royale) Act, which posits that, each year, a randomly chosen class of teenagers is carted off to an unpopulated island, given a map and compass, three days' rations and a just as randomly chosen weapon (some get a gun or axe, others a paper fan or pair of opera glasses). They are then left to get on with killing each other. Just as an incentive, tracking devices are fixed to their necks. These also contain an explosive charge. If the 'game' (rules: last child standing is the winner) is not concluded within the allotted three days, everyone's necklet is triggered.

Class B, the current crop of 15-year-old unfortunates, turn out not to be too bad a bunch for the most part. Nanahara (Tatsuya Fujiwara) is living with the trauma of his father's suicide, but with his girlfriend Noriko (Aki Maeda) as friend and confidante, he has remained well balanced. Many of the other teens have normal lives. 'I wanted a marriage,' one girl says as she lies dying, 'to grow old naturally, like my mother.' There are, of course, rotten apples in the barrel. Bitchy narcissist Mitsuko (Kou Shibasaki) turns out to be as proficient with a variety of weapons as she is with beauty products. A couple of older, more athletic transfer students, Kiriyama (Masanobu Ando) and Kawada (Taro Yamamoto), give cause for concern. Kiriyama is established from the outset as a fully fledged psychopath, even by Mitsuko's bloodthirsty standards. Kawada, on the other hand, is revealed as a survivor of an earlier game, forced in the final moments to kill his girlfriend, who becomes a guardian angel to Nanahara and Noriko.

The three days Class B spend on the island unfolds as a series of graphic vignettes. The deaths – and there are many; only two

Petty rivalries explode into violence in *Battle Royale*

characters make it through to the closing credits – are alternately arbitrary, disturbing and poignant. The first victim expires from a crossbow bolt through the neck within seconds of the game beginning. Mitsuko's attack (with a stun gun) on a classmate who, terrified, has turned to her for comfort, is chilling. Later, Mitsuko's death at the hands of Kiriyama, played out to Bach's 'Air on the G String'[7], is strangely poetic; certainly more elegiac than she deserves.

A strand of gallows humour is evident throughout, as in the coterie of giggling girls, still primly attired in their uniforms, whose coy bantering suddenly spirals into a Tarantinoesque Mexican stand-off when jealousy intrudes. The sudden transition is comedic – until the bullet-riddled payoff reminds us that none of their deaths were necessary. Elsewhere, other emotions are piqued: a young couple form a suicide pact rather than be party to violence. Alliances are formed. A group of computer nerds, one of whom boasts that his uncle was involved in reactionary politics in the Sixties, mount a counter-attack on the military installation whose staff (led by former teacher Kitano [Beat Takeshi], himself a victim of teen violence) are monitoring proceedings. Sadly, their campaign is scuppered when the shotgun-touting Kiriyama destroys their stronghold.

Kiriyama is finally defeated by Kawada, who then fakes Nanahara and Noriko's deaths to dupe the authorities. Kitano, remaining on the island after the military has left, finds himself confronted by the threesome. He provokes his own death by pulling a gun on them (it turns out to be a water pistol). The teenagers leave the island by boat. Kawada dies en route from wounds sustained during his duel with Kiriyama. Nanahara and Noriko return to the mainland only to find themselves criminals – wanted, absurdly, for murder.

For all that *Battle Royale* is an upsetting film (most of its duration is occupied by scenes of children killing or being killed), its most disturbing element is the role played by the adult world. Class B are chosen utterly at random. They are forced to adhere to a set of rules, never mind how heinous the 'game'; a dissenter has his head blown off when Kitano triggers his necklet before the contest has even begun. Yet Kitano, supposedly an observer as events unfold of their own accord, intercedes at one point to save favourite pupil Noriko.

Not that he does her any favours. When she and Narahara make it home – or at least, back to the city that used to be their home – it is as fugitives, on the run, faced with the impossibility of re-integration into a world that has forever been betrayed and corrupted by the forces of adulthood.

amorality and anti-heroism

When, at the end of World War II, French critics began reviewing the first American films they had seen in over six years, they noticed how much more shadowy and cynical they had become; how dark. This was partly due to the very different sensibilities society had after the war, and partly to the influx of European expressionist filmmakers into Hollywood, fleeing Nazi tyranny. The French critics coined a term to denote this new, harsher style of cinema: film noir.

Dark cinema: sex, death and cynicism in film noir

It is fitting that a genre so concerned with sleaze, its protagonists moving through a neon nightscape of disreputable locations peopled with brutal thugs and loose (often duplicitous) *femmes fatales*, found its inspiration in the pages of hard-boiled pulp fiction. The vivid prose of Raymond Chandler, James Hadley Chase, Dashiell Hammett and James M Cain transferred well to the big screen.

As we have seen with the spaghetti western, personal gain is the chief motivational factor in the genre – that is when its protagonists aren't simply looking for oblivion or, to quote a line from **High Sierra** (Raoul Walsh, 1941), 'rushing towards death'. Walsh's film marks a transition from the crime-film-as-morality-play ethos of pre-war Hollywood (Michael Curtiz's *Angels with Dirty Faces* [1938], for example). It also made a star of Humphrey Bogart, who invests his character, Roy 'Mad Dog' Earle, with the rumpled melancholy that made him a natural for *Casablanca* (Curtiz, 1942).

Earle is a heist merchant, newly released from jail. Teaming up with a couple of younger hoods (Alan Curtis and Arthur Kennedy), he finds that things have changed and his methods are outmoded. Friction with his partners is exacerbated by the presence of the slatternly Marie (Ida Lupino), moll to one of them. Walsh presupposes the gangster's moll/nice girl juxtaposition that would quickly become a genre cliché when Earle later becomes involved with a hick country family whose daughter Velma (Joan Leslie) is clubfooted – then turns the tables by having Velma turn her back on Earle as soon as he's paid for her operation. Marie, the only friend Earle has by the end of the film, is nonetheless the unwitting agent of his demise. Holed up in the mountains, pinned down by police, Marie is instructed by detectives to reason with him, to persuade him to surrender. When he reveals himself during their exchange, a marksman coldly guns him down.

Although the violence in *High Sierra* is tame, the blurring of moral lines and the grim sense of inevitability make it an important film noir milestone. The same year, Bogart was cast as Sam Spade in **The Maltese Falcon** (1941), John Huston's adaptation of Dashiell Hammett's novel[1]. The film is dark and claustrophobic. Apart from a montage of exteriors during the opening credits that set the scene as San Francisco, the action mainly takes place in the tightly composed interiors of offices and hotel rooms. Violence is part of the fabric of the film. Spade knocks around an effete dandy (Peter Lorre), telling him 'when you're slapped, you'll take it and like it' (machismo/homophobia). He gets the edge on a 'heavy' (whom he later mocks as a 'pocket edition desperado') by pulling his jacket off his shoulders, constricting his arms so that he cannot defend himself as Spade knocks him out. Later, when the corpulent and not-very-tactfully named Kasper Gutman (Sydney Greenstreet) spikes his drink, the heavy settles the score, kicking Spade in the face as he falls to the floor. Mary Astor's *femme fatale* is no less dangerous, using lies and promises of love to try to make Spade take the fall for her. (Atypical of film noir: men use guns as a weapon; women use sex – or at least, the promise thereof.)

Humphrey Bogart as cynical private eye Sam Spade in *The Maltese Falcon*

The film pays off with a line that, in its rejection of conventional morality, typifies the genre. The eponymous statuette, valuable enough that murder has been committed in the pursuit of it, is returned to the authorities by Spade – who is no better off at the end of the case and whose partner has been killed. 'What is it?' one of the officers asks. 'The stuff that dreams are made of,' he replies. It is a bitter and cynical line, but then such stuff is at the heart of film noir. The bitterness is at the arbitrariness of fate – what the Victorian poet Henley called 'the bludgeonings of chance'[2] – while the cynicism comes in the portrayal of human relationships, manipulation and fallibility.

Cynicism about relationships is demonstrated by male culpability in the likes of *Double Indemnity* (Billy Wilder, 1944) and *The Postman Always Rings Twice* (Tay Garnett, 1946), the latter from James M Cain's novel. Both share similar plots: a weak-willed man is seduced by a scheming *femme fatale* into participating in the murder of the latter's husband. The lovers in **Out of the Past** (aka *Build My Gallows High*, Jacques Tourneur, 1947) play an even more dangerous game. Rumpled private eye Jeff Bailey (Robert Mitchum, in a role that did for him what *High Sierra* did for Bogart) cuckolds mobster Whit Sterling (Kirk Douglas) by accepting the favours of his moll, Kathie Moffett (Jane Greer). Moffett has already enraged Sterling by absconding with $40,000 of his ill-gotten gains, and he employs Bailey to find her. Moffett leads the smitten Bailey into a series of increasingly tangled misdeeds, culminating when she betrays him following a robbery he commits at her behest. Discovering her treachery, Bailey responds (and seals his own fate) by tipping off the police as to their whereabouts: attempting to escape, they are gunned down at a roadblock. (In addition to this bullet-riddled finale, *Out of the Past* boasts one of the most inventive death scenes in film noir, when a fishing line snags one of Sterling's thugs and yanks him off a high promontory.) Sex and death go hand in hand, chaperoned by greed and duplicity. Men are shown in a poor light, easily duped; women come off just as badly, objectified as voluptuous manipulators.

For all its inherent nastiness, the spirit of film noir endures. Adaptations of pulp novelist Jim Thompson's work are scattered across three decades of film production, from Peckinpah's *The Getaway* (1972) – remade in 1994 by Roger Donaldson – to Stephen Frears's *The Grifters* (1990). Recently, *Bound* (Andy and Larry Wachowski, 1996) has contemporized the sexuality of film noir by having a bisexual gangster's moll and her lesbian lover swindle the mob.

The 1970s: death of the American dream

Film noir is not, of course, the only example of an era of filmmaking defined by its social context. If film noir demonstrated a darker aesthetic, then the films of the Seventies – surely one of the most astounding decades in the history of American cinema – spelled out the death of the American dream and gave voice to a disaffected generation.

Although American involvement in Vietnam had begun as early as 1955, it was a decade later that the conflict escalated; it played out under the glare of the world's media for another decade. The war was a military embarrassment and an economic disaster for the government. It marked a turning point in the faith of the people in their leaders, a disaffection that reached its zenith with the Watergate scandal in 1972 and Richard Nixon's resignation from the White House two years later.

The Sixties had ended badly: in August 1969, followers of Charles Manson committed a grisly multiple murder in the heart of Los Angeles (one of the victims was actress Sharon Tate, pregnant with the child of director Roman Polanski); in December of the same year, at the Altamont Speedway rock concert headlined by the Rolling Stones, the Hell's Angels who were supposedly providing security knifed a young black man, killing him. The ideal of peace and love was over. The violence of Manson's acolytes and the Hell's Angels was reflected in the television images of Vietnam. Social discontent was rife. Protestors burned the flag.

Naturally, filmmakers reacted. **Bonnie and Clyde** (Arthur Penn, 1967) had already depicted its titular outlaws as folk heroes; role models, even. When Bonnie Parker (Faye Dunaway) tells an awe-struck onlooker, 'we rob banks', it is almost a calling card from a new generation of filmmakers (Scorsese, Coppola, de Palma, et al. would emerge in the next few years) saying 'we question the system'.

Cinema became blatantly anti-establishment. Crime films showed police officers employing methods no different to their criminal counterparts. In *Dirty Harry*, Callaghan's shoot-first-ask-questions-later attitude alienates him from his superiors. The other members of his precinct, faceless and ineffectual, represent the 'system' that he has to circumvent in order to get results. When, having dispatched the Scorpio Killer, he throws his badge away, it is a rejection of the bureaucratic system in which a maverick (i.e. an individual) will always be hampered.

Even a film based on an actual case, the seizure of heroin with a street value of $32 million (at the time, the biggest ever narcotics bust), came across less as a celebration of a successful police operation than a documentary-style account of shambolic officers existing on a diet of junk food and obsessive hatred of their prey. **The French Connection** (William Friedkin, 1971) starts with 'Popeye' Doyle (Gene Hackman) on a stakeout. Dressed in a Santa Claus outfit, he chases down a suspect and beats out of him the information he

Rogue justice: Doyle (Gene Hackman) makes his 'arrest' in *The French Connection*

wants. (Kathryn Bigelow's *Strange Days* [1995] uses a similar image to make the same point about the breakdown of traditional social values: here, the individual dressed as Santa is being set upon by a street gang.) Later, fired upon by a hitman working for his nemesis, drug baron Charnier (Fernando Rey), Doyle pursues the assassin in a high-speed chase that endangers the lives of any number of motorists and pedestrians (he even appropriates a car, more or less at gunpoint). Doyle catches up with him; when the hitman makes a last-ditch attempt to escape, fleeing up the steps to an elevated train station, Doyle shoots him in the back.

He's just as destructive a force around his own kind. He punches out an informant, ostensibly to prevent his cover being blown – but he doesn't pull the punch! He gets into a fight with a fellow officer, Mulderig (Bill Hickman), who has been harassing him about the death of a colleague, which Doyle may or may not have been responsible for on a previous job. This conflict is resolved in a truly disturbing final scene. Doyle and his team take down the criminals at an abandoned factory where Charnier has been closing the deal. Charnier escapes, leaving Doyle scouring the disused and low-lit building in search of him. He sees a figure through a doorway and fires. His partner, Buddy Russo (Roy Scheider) joins him as they make their way over to identify the body. It's Mulderig. Russo is aghast, but Doyle registers no emotion. Still obsessed with finding Charnier, he charges off into another part of the factory, firing at nothing. This is where the film ends – the closing credits denote the

52

relatively low sentences handed down to those arrested – leaving one to wonder how 'accidental' the shooting of Mulderig was.

The French Connection goes further than *Dirty Harry*. Callaghan, for all that he discards his badge, is ultimately vindicated, saving a bus full of schoolchildren held hostage by the Scorpio Killer. His methods may be dubious, but he still does the right thing. Doyle, however, finds no vindication: the criminal mastermind who was behind the drugs ring escapes, and Doyle's motives are thrown into even greater doubt.

Eschewing the abrasiveness of Siegel and Friedkin's films for a more satirical approach, Joseph Sargent's **The Taking of Pelham 123** (1974) has the police as a token presence, sidelined while the mayor of New York dithers, leaving laconic Transit Authority Inspector Garber (Walter Matthau) to save the day when an armed gang take a subway train and its passengers hostage. Hence the 'system' is literal (the New York transit system) as well as metaphorical (the government). Sargent also establishes effective contrasts between the lax behaviour of Garber's co-workers and the indecision of the mayor and his entourage, inviting us to laugh at the inefficiency on display whatever the system and whomever is in charge.

The violence is no laughing matter, though. The criminals (who identify each other only by colours – a device Tarantino pays homage to in *Reservoir Dogs*) are indiscriminate in their use of force: they stipulate that one hostage be killed every hour until the $1 million ransom is paid – and waste no time in proving that they are serious. Their leader, Mr Blue (Robert Shaw), places just as little value on his own life when Garber gets the drop on him.

> **Mr Blue:** Excuse me, do you people still execute in this state?
> **Garber:** What? Execute? Not at the moment.
> **Mr Blue:** Pity.

And so saying, he steps on the electrified central rail.

Railways make for an equally violent milieu in **Emperor of the North** (Aldrich, 1973), which dresses up its anti-authoritarian ethos in grungy period garb. The system is represented by Shack (Ernest Borgnine), a guard pathologically opposed to anyone getting a free ride; the individual by A-Number One (Lee Marvin), a colourfully named hobo. In fact, the hoboes, with their long hair and commune-based 'underground' society, can be seen as a stand-in for the hippie/student element opposed to Nixon and deeply critical of the

American political system. The finale has A–Number One and Shack go *mano-a-mano* in an open wagon as the train thunders through the wilderness, using hammers, chains and lengths of wood in a no-holds-barred fight.

For all of A–Number One's rough and ready charm, and his victory over the establishment when he throws Shack from the train, *Emperor of the North* is freighted with a cynical subtext: the train represents transport/industrialization, the implements the combatants fight with are tools and building materials. Here we have a metaphor for economic progress, subverted by a freeloader.

Aesthetically, with its steam locomotive, country-and-western soundtrack and traditional showdown, *Emperor of the North* is very much a western and, as we have seen, violence in cinema is often congenital to genre. The gangster film, one of the most popular offshoots of the crime drama, spawned two of the greatest films of the Seventies: *The Godfather* and *The Godfather Part II* and. These films attain a mythic quality even as they destroy value systems wholesale.

Strictly business: honour, betrayal and violence in the gangster film

Early on in ***The Godfather*** (Coppola, 1972), Don Corleone (Marlon Brando) tells the loose-tongued Sonny (James Caan) 'never let anyone outside the family know what you're thinking'. Establishing from its very first scenes an image of the Sicilian family as close-knit and patriarchal, the film embraces this concept of unity and kinship wholeheartedly. But it is a skewed vision. Sonny and his adopted brother Tom Hagen (Robert Duvall) have followed the Don into the family business (criminality), while Michael (Al Pacino) is considered the black sheep of the family for enlisting with the Marines. Already, the conventional hero (rejecting criminality to serve his country) has become the most nominal of family members, all but sidelined at his sister's wedding celebrations, the extended set piece with which the film begins.

The lines are blurred even further when Michael, in response to the shooting and hospitalization of his father, proposes and successfully executes the assassination of Sollozzo (Al Lettieri), the mobster responsible for the actions against the Don, and Captain McCluskey (Sterling Hayden), the corrupt police officer who has assisted him. Never mind that he is the black sheep: because of his concept of 'family' he makes the transition from decorated war hero to double murderer with disturbing ease. Obliged to take a sabbatical in Sicily to evade US authorities, he deserts his girlfriend Kay (Diane Keaton), compounding his betrayal of her when he marries local beauty Apollonia (Simonetta Stefanelli). His sojourn culminates in Apollonia's death in a car bomb intended for him, and Michael returns to America and blithely resumes his relationship with Kay.

In the meantime, Sonny has been betrayed by the brother-in-law to whom he administers a beating (utilizing a baseball bat and the lid of a galvanized dustbin) in retribution for his tendency to wife-beating. The elder son dead and the Don having reluctantly made peace with his enemies, the family business is turned over to Michael. With the Don's retirement (and his death shortly afterwards), all traces of honour – familial or otherwise – are overturned. Michael, at the outset the one member of the Corleone clan least tainted by crime, degenerates into remorseless villainy, alternately lying to and intimidating his wife, orchestrating the deaths of the heads of the 'Five Families' (the Corleones' competition in the criminal underworld) and ordering the death of his brother-in-law. He moves from hero to anti-hero in one classic movie.

The sins of the father: Michael Corleone (Al Pacino) inherits the family business

Perversely, it is Michael's very coldness, his lack of emotionalism, which facilitates his ascendancy to the head of the Corleone family. Sonny, by comparison, is the victim of his emotions: hearing of another beating sustained by his sister (Talia Shire), he tears off to her aid without waiting for his bodyguards. Ambushed at a toll-booth en route, his car is riddled with machine-gun fire. Michael's reactions are calculated; even when he vengefully suggests the hit on Sollozzo and McCluskey, he works out an angle whereby Corleone contacts in the media can exploit the policeman's dirty dealings. 'It's not personal,' is Michael's credo, 'it's strictly business.' Ironically, these were Sollozzo's words to him following the attempt on the Don's life.

Such vestiges as are left of Michael's humanity are lost in **The**

Godfather Part II (Coppola, 1974). The narrative is structured to contrast the rise to power of the young Don Corleone (Robert de Niro) with Michael's barren life. In short: the father's development of the business and the son's misuse of it. The Don's actions, though criminal, are beneficent: when he kills a neighbourhood crime boss, it is to the betterment of the community's quality of life. Michael's actions, however, bring ruination to all concerned. Family values are negated at every turn. Michael responds to the threat of testimony against him in a court of law by inveigling the companionship of the witness's father, the implicit threat of violence against the old man ensuring a change of heart under cross-examination. Kay,

Blood ties? Al Pacino and John Cazale as brothers divided in *The Godfather Part II*

increasingly alienated, finally leaves him after revealing that the loss of their second child, originally thought to be a miscarriage, was an act of termination on her part: 'It wasn't a miscarriage. It was an abortion. An abortion, Michael. Just like our marriage is an abortion. Something that's unholy and evil. I didn't want your son, Michael. I wouldn't bring another one of your sons into this world … I had it killed because this must all end … this Sicilian thing that's been going on for two thousand years.'

For all the generic violence of the film – shootings, stabbings, garrottings – this scene, Kay's soliloquy curtailed by the blow Michael deals her, is truly horrifying: a mother admitting to the abortion of her unborn child rather than bring it into a family whose ethics have become this devalued.

And still there is one final unconscionable act. Michael's surviving brother, the weak-willed Fredo (John Cazale), betrays him over an ultimately disastrous bid for casino operation in Cuba (American interests, legal or otherwise, are nullified by the revolution). Fredo, perpetually unable to hold his own, trusts the wrong people and is easily manipulated. Michael waits until the death of their mother (i.e. until the last connection to the old way of doing things is severed), feigns forgiveness of his brother, welcomes him back into the household, then orders his execution. For all the deaths he has been a party to, it is this act of fratricide that places him beyond redemption[3].

A more 'working class' vision of organized crime, where betrayal is an occupational hazard and violence flares up at the drop of a hat, is evinced by Martin Scorsese. **Mean Streets** (1973) is set in the tenement buildings, bars and back rooms of Little Italy. None of the opulence of the Corleones is on display. There are no glitzy casinos or high-stake deals. The only similarity is in the sense of Catholic guilt that shadows the film. Charlie (Harvey Keitel), a young man on the fringes of crime by dint of his uncle's line in running numbers, is introduced in a voiceover communicating his thoughts over a black screen: 'You don't make up for your sins in church. You do it on the streets; you do it in your homes. The rest is bullshit and you know it.'[4]

Charlie's days are spent collecting protection payments, socializing in a grotty bar and keeping an eye out for his emotionally insecure friend Johnny Boy (Robert de Niro). His sense of guilt is exacerbated by the affair he is secretly having with Johnny Boy's cousin Teresa (Amy Robinson). In a rare interlude with Teresa, as they walk along the beach, Charlie tells her, 'I hate the ocean and I hate the beach and I hate the sun and the grass and the trees.' *Mean Streets*, like *The Godfather*, is a film without heroes. But unlike Coppola's film, there is no mythicism, no sense of a great saga being played out. The only code of honour Charlie subscribes to is his friendship, however one-sided it may be, with Johnny Boy, a wastrel who accrues gambling debts and makes a dangerous enemy of loan shark Michael (Richard Romanus). This conflict is resolved after Johnny Boy threatens Michael with a revolver. Disarming Johnny Boy after Michael has departed, Charlie makes one last play for his friend's salvation, insisting on driving him out of town until he has had a chance to placate Michael. But it is salvation denied. Michael and hitman Shorty (Scorsese) shoot Johnny Boy in a drive-by, an act that also leaves Charlie and Teresa badly injured.

This scene apart, much of the violence is apropos of nothing. A brawl breaks out as the friends sit talking in a bar, a venue at which a shooting later occurs – the patrons make a swift departure lest they be implicated. A skirmish takes place during an otherwise amicable payoff at a pool hall when Johnny Boy calls someone a 'mook'; notwithstanding that nobody knows what the word means – 'a mook, what's a mook?' – it is taken as an insult and a fight ensues utilizing fists, feet and pool cues.

The same sense of arbitrariness permeates Scorsese's later film, ***GoodFellas*** (1990), an account of the rise and fall of mobster Henry Hill (Ray Liotta), who turns evidence against his cohorts when the net tightens. Partners in Henry's criminal undertakings – robberies and drug deals – are Jimmy Conway (Robert de Niro) and Tommy DeVito (Joe Pesci), both older men who serve as mentors of a sort. Not that Tommy is anything of a role model. In an early scene, he verbally demolishes Henry. Holding court with a colourful account of a beating he once took from a cop, Tommy has Henry and a bunch of other hoods in hysterics. 'You're a funny guy,' Henry remarks, wiping away tears of laughter. Tommy rounds on him: 'Funny how? Funny like I'm a clown, like I amuse you? I make you laugh. Like I'm here to fucking amuse you? … What the fuck is so funny about me?'

GoodFellas: bad men looking cool in Scorsese's classic

Henry, pallid, musters enough nerve to call his bluff. 'You stuttering prick, you', Tommy abuses him: 'I worry about you sometimes. You may fold under questioning.'

It doesn't take long for Tommy's rage to manifest as physical violence, whether against a youthful bartender who is slow to serve a drink (Tommy shoots him in the foot, trying to replicate a scene in a western where a bartender is made to 'dance') and who later, foot bandaged and understandably peeved, invites him to 'go fuck yourself' (Tommy shoots him again, this time repeatedly in the chest). Or, in a more ill-considered incident, against 'made man' (i.e. someone of proven Sicilian ancestry who belongs to the Mob's inner circle) Billy Batts (Frank Vincent)[5]. A celebration after a profitable heist turns nasty when Billy wisecracks about Tommy's childhood, specifically how he worked as a shoe-shine boy. Tommy takes the bait, but Jimmy steps in to smooth things over. Billy turns away, but mouths a final insult: 'Now go home and get your fucking shinebox.' Tommy, rabid, has to be dragged out of the bar. Later in the evening he returns. Billy is still there, sharing drinks and reminiscences with Jimmy and Henry. They turn on him brutally. Henry locks the door while Tommy and Jimmy kick Billy half to death.

Driving out to the woods and a shallow grave, a thumping comes from the trunk. They pull over, open it, and find him still alive. Tommy sets about him with a carving knife, then Jimmy fires several shots into his already blood-drenched body. Henry – notwithstanding his proclivities towards violence (in an early scene he administers a merciless pistol-whipping) – throws up as they inter the corpse.

Ultimately, it is this act that buries them all: Tommy is whacked in revenge for Billy. Henry and Jimmy, ostracized from their former associates, enter into a badly planned series of drug deals. Both men become paranoid from overusing the goods they traffic in. Their lives spiral out of control. When Henry is arrested in a narcotics bust, he rats out everyone to save himself. The film ends with him living in bland anonymity courtesy of a witness-protection program. 'I get to live the rest of my life like a schmuck,' he complains, as if he deserved even a fragment of pity for the arrogance of his wasted existence.

The British crime film, if anything, is even more cynical and hard-edged, its gangsters moving through a world where friendship counts for nothing and betrayal is dispassionate in its matter-of-factness. ***Get Carter*** (Mike Hodges, 1971) opens with its eponymous anti-hero (Michael Caine), a London-based gangster, returning to Newcastle, the stamping ground of his youth. He is there to attend his brother's funeral – and to make sure someone pays for his sibling's death. What follows is essentially a hard-boiled detective story, but with a career criminal fulfilling the role of private eye. Carter uncovers a conspiracy centred around a blue movie racket. Already enraged by his brother's murder, he is driven to ever greater lengths when he discovers his niece has appeared in one of the pornographic films.

The business end of a shotgun:
Michael Caine in *Get Carter*

Carter enters the film alone, and alone he walks through the industrial landscape of his long-forsaken hometown. His loyalty to his paymasters back in London is questionable: he is cuckolding one of his bosses, carrying on an affair with his moll (Britt Ekland). In Newcastle, he is friendless. The one person who helps him in his quest – Keith (Alun Armstrong), a friend of his brother – he uses, then leaves to take a beating on his account. In a scene that speaks volumes about his callousness, Carter visits him afterwards; the young man is confined to bed, his face a welter of bruises. Carter peels a few notes from a bankroll and tosses them at him. 'Get yourself some karate lessons,' he advises, and leaves.

Elsewhere, bracing corrupt property dealer Brumby (Bryan Mosley), Carter responds to the man's brusque protestations by informing him, 'You're a big man, but you're out of shape. I do this for a job.' Then he drops him with two swift blows. Later, discovering the true extent of Brumby's involvement, he beats him even more severely and throws him off a multi-storey car park. Brumby's body impacts on a car, flattening the roof. The horn sounds its single loud, flat note as spectators gather around and – in a scene often missing when *Get Carter* is screened on television – help to carry out the bodies of a woman and her daughter.

Everyone pays, no matter how great or little part they played. When Carter extracts the final piece of information from the peripherally involved Albert (Glynn Edwards), information that leads back to his old nemesis Eric Paice (Ian Hendry), he permits Albert a last cigarette, then pulls a flick-knife. On his knees, Albert pleads to no avail:

> **Albert:** Jack, for Christ's sake –
> **Carter:** You knew what I'd do, didn't you?
> **Albert:** Christ, I didn't kill him.
> **Carter:** I know you didn't kill him. [Carter stabs Albert] I know. [He stabs him again]

60

There is also a perverse sense of ceremony in Carter's revenge on Eric, whose own employer – local big-shot Kinnear (John Osborne) – sells him out to Carter. If Albert's shakily smoked last cigarette marks him out as a condemned man even before the switchblade glints in Carter's hand, the bottle of whisky extended to Eric is bleakly redolent of someone being offered 'one for the road'. Maybe 'offered' isn't the right word. Extended, yes – but at gunpoint. Brandishing a shotgun, Carter marches him out to a coastland that is more black than golden, more rubbish-dump than resort. An aerial ropeway carries buckets of colliery spoil out to sea where they are dumped, the empty buckets then rattling back inland. It is against their inexorable rotation that Carter forces Eric to ingest the scotch, then clubs him to death with the butt of the shotgun.

Everyone pays – and that includes Carter. He loads Eric's body on one of the buckets, laughs as he watches it deposited in a black slurry into the sea, then sets off along the beach, pausing only to hurl the shotgun into the dreary waters. A shot rings out and Carter falls, dead. The assassin – hired by Kinnear and glimpsed in the credits sequence sitting across from Carter in the railway carriage that carries him back to Newcastle – strips down his rifle and strolls unhurriedly away. The tide laps at Carter's body as it rolls slowly in.

Power structures and betrayal – not to mention the inevitability of there always being a bigger operator – are central to **The Long Good Friday** (John MacKenzie, 1979). Harold Shand (Bob Hoskins) is a London crime boss who has carved himself an empire. He lives the life of a playboy: Rolls-Royce, yacht, glamorous trophy wife (Helen Mirren). As the film opens he is lining up a business deal with Mafia representatives over from America. Over the course of Easter weekend, an escalating wave of attacks are directed against him: his Roller is destroyed in a car-bomb that almost kills his mother; his oldest friend and most trusted associate is stabbed; a bomb is planted in his casino; and a pub he owns, the Lion and Unicorn, is gutted in an explosion just as he drives up outside with his mob cohorts.

His attempts to determine who is responsible are equally violent. He solicits from a corrupt police inspector the name of his most reliable informant. Paying him a visit, Harold and his boys pull the unfortunate man naked from his bed and slash his buttocks with a machete until they realize that his repeated assertion that he knows nothing is in fact true. Nor does brute force get him any further when he pulls in every 'face who works his manor' (in English, every known criminal who operates on his territory), and has them hung upside down from meat-hooks in an abattoir, threatening them with the rest of the night in the cold store if they don't talk. Again, he is quick to realize that none of them are in on it, and he is forced to pay them off ('a grand apiece for expenses') and turn them loose.

There is a similar scene in John Boorman's *The General* (1998), a biopic of Martin Cahill (Brendan Gleeson), an apolitical Irish professional criminal: concerned that one of his men is skimming off the top, Cahill crucifies him on a pool table. When the youth, whimpering in pain, persists in pleading his innocence, Cahill realizes his mistake. The lad is swiftly transported to hospital, and is soon thereafter seen to resume work in Cahill's organization. Boorman's film ends with Cahill, having taken one liberty too many, being assassinated by the IRA.

There is a similar ending in *The Long Good Friday*. By the time Harold learns the truth, he has been betrayed by one of his most trusted advisors, and made an enemy of the IRA. His deal with the Mafia is scuppered when they get cold feet over the amount of 'bombs going off everywhere … like Beirut on a bad night'. Harold responds by roundly abusing them: 'I've heard of sleeping partners, but you're in a fucking coma … Mafia? I've shit 'em!' It is on this note of monstrous egoism that the film reaches its dark conclusion. Storming out on the Americans, Harold signals to his driver; the car pulls round and he climbs in. It roars off at speed and Harold finds himself held at gunpoint, helpless, by IRA men. For all his phoney patriotism (his vision of a new London, his veneration of British culture and sophistication; the way he berates the Americans for not having any 'Dunkirk spirit'), he is brought down not by another criminal fraternity (the Mafia representatives are circumspect and businesslike) or by the authorities (he buys off high-ranking coppers), but by a terrorist organization whose agenda is publicly anti-British.

View from the dark side: the lure of evil

The development of the villain recast as hero is illustrated by one of modern cinema's most popular characters: Hannibal Lecter. It was the success of Jonathan Demme's **The Silence of the Lambs** (1990) that made the cultured serial killer a household name, as well as sweeping the board at the Oscars. Although it is with Anthony

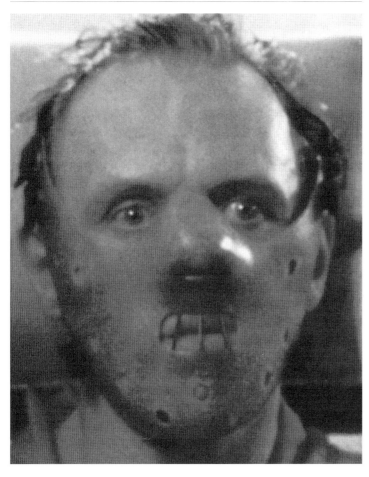

Anthony Hopkins as Hannibal Lecter in *The Silence of the Lambs*

Hopkins that Lecter is immediately associated in the popular consciousness, the role was originally essayed by Brian Cox in **Manhunter** (Michael Mann, 1986). Adapted from Thomas Harris's novel *Red Dragon* (the title, apparently, was changed over concern that audiences would consider it a martial arts picture), there are distinct parallels between the plots of *Manhunter* and *The Silence of the Lambs*. Both have troubled protagonists – Will Graham (William Peterson), a psychological profiler disturbed by his ability to fathom the minds of sociopaths, and Clarice Starling (Jodie Foster), a trainee FBI agent haunted by childhood trauma. Both centre around the hunt for psychologically motivated serial killers – the Tooth Fairy (so called because of the bite marks he leaves and the lack of sexual interference with his female victims); and Buffalo Bill (because he 'skins his humps'). And, crucially, both require their protagonists to seek the help of the incarcerated Lecter[6]. The portrayal of Lecter, however, couldn't be more different.

In *Manhunter*, Lecter is peripheral, his help reluctantly sought by Graham – reluctantly, because Graham was responsible for Lecter's imprisonment. Back-story reveals that Lecter brutally attacked Graham before he could facilitate the serial killer's arrest. It is the physical as well as psychological damage done to Graham that makes him abandon his work as a profiler; when the film opens, he is brought out of 'retirement' when no-one else can make headway with the Tooth Fairy case.

Graham visits Lecter at a maximum security psychiatric institution. His cell is small and sparse, decorated in clinical white. So, too, is Lecter cold; unemotional. Cox plays him with an impassivity underpinned by a sense of boredom, as if the likes of Graham are simply too tiresome. Lecter toys with him intellectually, incisively probing Graham's troubled psyche while revealing nothing of himself. Later, he attempts revenge on Graham by communicating with the Tooth Fairy – from within his cell – sending a coded message which contains Graham's home address and urges the Tooth Fairy to kill his family. His ploy is ultimately unsuccessful – the message is intercepted, decoded and the Graham family evacuated – but it demonstrates Lecter's ruthlessness, intellectualism and talent for manipulation.

Lecter is again approached for help in the apprehension of another serial killer in *The Silence of the Lambs*, but this time the dialectic is different. Firstly, Starling is a woman and as Dr Chiltern (Anthony Heald) – the director of the institute – points out, it has been several years since Lecter has seen a woman. Added to the element of flirtation, there is a sense of Lecter establishing himself as a sort of mentor to Starling. He is an older man; he quickly finds out that Starling's father, a man she idolized, died when she was young. He seems to be stepping into the breach, alternately reprimanding and encouraging her at each of their encounters. Secondly, unlike Graham, there is no previous connection between them; no history. As a rookie – still in training to become an agent – Starling as yet poses no threat to him.

Accordingly, the film's aesthetic has an element of the gothic. Lecter's cell is subterranean, hewn out of rock. Thus he becomes a darkly romantic figure, seductive yet sinister, hidden from the light of the world. One can easily equate him with such fictive antecedents as Dracula and the Phantom of the Opera. Likewise, Starling is akin to the heroines of gothic fantasy, albeit not so willowy and a lot more capable with a handgun. Three times during the course of the film she ventures alone into dark and potentially dangerous places: the troglodytic section of the institute where Lecter is kept (past the cell belonging to the sexually perverted Miggs); the storage facility where she discovers the head of one of Lecter's victims; and the basement where Buffalo Bill is holding his latest captive. She enters into a relationship with Lecter, providing him with information about herself in return for his input on the Buffalo Bill case. This is a twisted version of courtship, with Lecter, in essence, getting to know her better. Thus, the portrayal of Lecter differs from *Manhunter*. Here, he is charming and cultured. Even when he denigrates Starling's social background ('you're not more than one generation removed from poor white trash'), he does so with an irony that is as much self-deprecation *vis-à-vis* his own snobbery. The disinterest he displays in *Manhunter* is replaced with a satirical and contemptuous amusement in *The Silence of the Lambs* and, in his scenes with Starling, with a wry affection.

Lecter's role in *Manhunter* is hardly pro-active. Even when he endangers Graham's family, he has to manipulate other people: telephonists in order to obtain information on Graham; the Tooth Fairy to act in his stead. In *The Silence of the Lambs* his presence is more prominent, his role most certainly pro-active. True, his talent for manipulation remains undiminished: after Miggs's unspeakable behaviour towards Starling (he masturbates and throws his semen at her), Lecter convinces him to end his life. ('The orderly heard Lecter whispering to him all afternoon and Miggs crying,' Starling is informed. 'At bed check, they found him. He'd swallowed his own tongue.') He takes a more hands-on approach, though, while he is being transferred to another facility under the terms of an agreement with the senator whose daughter has been abducted by Buffalo Bill. The murder of his two guards is brutal. He bludgeons one to death with his own truncheon, and crucifies and eviscerates the other. His means of escape, disguising himself in a dead man's skin to inveigle an ambulance ride away from the scene, is gruesome.

Yet, at the conclusion, Lecter has become if not a likeable character then certainly a darkly appealing one. His promise not to go after Starling as long as she extends him the same courtesy further romanticizes him. His singling out of an unsuspecting Dr Chiltern (already depicted unsympathetically for his impropriety towards Starling and his attempts to exploit the Buffalo Bill case to his own ends) for his return to the cuisine of human flesh – 'I'm having an old friend for dinner' – seals the film with a blackly comic pay-off line.

Dark humour is evident in Ridley Scott's **Hannibal** (2001). Lecter's cannibalism is treated lightly: his use of a discordant flautist as the main course at a dinner party is described as 'a public service … he did it to improve the sound of the Baltimore Philharmonic Orchestra'.

His sociopathic behaviour is dispensed within the first half hour: an attack on a nurse at a psychiatric hospital (shown as security tape footage), and a flashback to the disfigurement of Mason Verger (Gary Oldman), the film's nominal villain. Thereafter, his use of violence is retributive and motivated either by romanticism (against those who have done ill to Starling) or self-preservation (against the washed-up Italian police officer who tries to sell him out to Verger). It is Verger's attempts to trace the whereabouts, effect the capture of and take his revenge upon Lecter that provide the narrative. Even so, the film takes pains both to paint Verger as evil (he is a paedophile, and practises auto-eroticism), and to downplay Lecter's accountability: when Verger peels his own face off with a shard of glass, it is only at Lecter's suggestion. (Verger himself muses at one point that 'it seemed like a good idea at the time'.) While this maintains a certain continuity in terms of Lecter's skill in manipulating people – communicating with the Tooth Fairy, talking Miggs into killing himself – it does allow the filmmakers to elicit audience empathy: Verger is so irredeemably depraved that Lecter's removal of him from any social spectrum (he is rendered a bed-ridden recluse) is surely all to the good.

Romanticizing the villain: promotional artwork for *Hannibal*

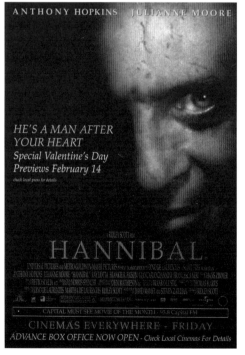

The sick nature of Verger's character makes villain of victim, and with Starling still every inch the beleaguered heroine – under internal investigation, her career threatened by Paul Krendler (Ray Liotta), a justice department bigwig whose advances she has spurned – the path is clear for Lecter to emerge as the romantic hero by default. His artistic preferences are emphasized throughout: he enjoys the splendours of Rome, lectures on art, reads poetry, and plays the piano[7]. His room is filled with *objets d'art*. The overall impression is of a refined, sensitive, intelligent and well-mannered individual – who just happens to enjoy eating people.

Which is not to say that *Hannibal* skimps on gore: Lecter disembowels Pazzi, the hapless Italian detective, hanging him from a balcony in homage to a 15th-century execution (Pazzi's mobile phone impacts on the cobblestones beneath, followed swiftly by his viscera); he knifes a would-be pickpocket (working in collusion with Pazzi to obtain information for Verger) in the groin; and – most spectacularly –he 'entertains' Krendler at dinner, performing a trepanation in order to serve him lightly sautéed portions of his own brain. The disposal of Verger, feasted on by the wild boars he'd intended to serve Lecter to, is equally graphic, but is again dissociative. He simply suggests to Verger's put-upon private physician that he might consider tipping his employer into their pen. The final act of violence is self-inflicted and reaffirms Lecter's romantic hero credentials. Handcuffed by Starling, the police closing in, he severs his hand at the wrist with a cleaver rather than harm her[8].

A killing at the box office: violence as entertainment

If the Seventies were a time of cinematic disaffection, then the preceding decade was driven by a different dialectic. The ethos of the Sixties was free love, social and cultural revolution. Fashion altered irreversibly; image became crucial. The concept of 'chic' was born. Youth gave itself an identity, while the paranoia of Cold War politics churned away in the background. It was in the early years of this decade that the novels of espionage writer Ian Fleming made their transition to the silver screen.

James Bond: Agent 007, licence to kill. One of the most popular fictional characters ever. He was suave, elegant, debonair, not to mention a techno-geek (the obligatory gadgets save his bacon each time he walks into another obvious trap), and misogynist (women are sexual playthings, turned to for R&R at the completion of a mission but dumped as soon as he's called back to the fray). Although frequently coy in their treatment of the subject, the Bond films are founded upon the twin adolescent fixations of sex and violence. Of course, it never gets too explicit in either department: the most stringent rating a Bond movie has yet received is a 15[9]. Nonetheless, the violence is often notable if for no other reason than the blithe manner in which it is represented.

It was the third instalment, ***Goldfinger*** (Guy Hamilton, 1964) that fully established the formula: gadgets (the Aston Martin DB5 'with modifications'), a villain with a gimmick (Oddjob and his steel-rimmed bowler hat), an improbably named heroine (Honor Blackman as the less-than-subtly monickered Pussy Galore), and a plot that serves merely as an excuse for scenic globetrotting. The pre-credits sequence (a non-sequitur as far as narrative is concerned) is also present and correct and provides a good example of amoral mainstream film violence: Bond (Sean Connery) emerges from an oily black lake, wetsuit dripping. He breaches a military installation and plants explosives. This done, Bond peels off the wetsuit to reveal a miraculously immaculate tuxedo. He repairs to a local bar where a scantily clad dancer is performing an exotic routine. Her gyrations cease as the explosion resounds; the regulars run outside to investigate. Bond conducts a whispered conversation with his contact, then follows the dancer into her dressing room where she is reclining in a bath. Bond makes his move; they embrace (she wears a towel; 007 takes off no more than his shoulder holster). Reflected in her eye, he sees an assassin creeping towards him, cosh in hand. He uses the girl as a shield (she is knocked unconscious – a pointer towards the even more ignominious fate suffered by Shirley Eaton in the film's key image). During the ensuing fight, Bond hurls the assassin into the bath. The man sees Bond's gun within easy reach and

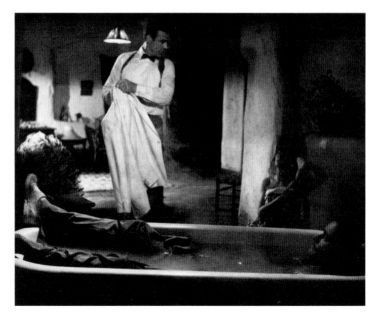

'Shocking, positively shocking':
Bond (Sean Connery)
despatches an antagonist

grabs at it. Bond seizes a conveniently placed one-bar electric fire and, in a scene that is still trimmed when the film is shown on terrestrial television, hurls it into the water. 'Shocking,' he quips as his screaming antagonist still twitches, 'positively shocking.'

As risible as the material is, the filmmakers organize it with a cynical cleverness worthy of any of 007's megalomaniac nemeses, with the end result of making it seem iconic. When Bond kills his antagonist the audience is not asked to think about it: the him-or-me aspect excuses Bond's actions, the preceding imagery of explosions and seductive femininity assures us that this is the norm in Bond's world, and the throwaway one-liner gives us permission to laugh it off.

A similar mindset permeates most blockbusters, particularly those, like the Bond films, which have developed into a franchise. The *Die Hard* and *Lethal Weapon* films trade on big explosions, smart-alec one-liners and the unstoppable heroism of their protagonists, never mind how flawed they actually are (McClane is a reluctant hero at the best of times – almost a victim of circumstances – while Riggs, certainly in the original *Lethal Weapon*, has a bona fide death wish). The Stallone and Schwarzenegger action movies of the Eighties and early Nineties tread the same path, wrapping their violence up in jokey, amoral packages aimed squarely at a teenage audience. It is this kind of functionless, emotionally retarded product that has led many filmmakers to question, re-address and redefine the portrayal of violence, even at the risk of demonstrating a bleak and pessimistic worldview.

Nihilism and social disaffection

'You are not a beautiful and unique snowflake. You are the all-singing, all-dancing crap of this world.' Thus speaks Tyler Durden (Brad Pitt) in David Fincher's incendiary vision of urban nihilism **Fight Club** (1999). Durden is the alter ego of 'Jack' (Edward Norton), the film's narrator. 'Jack' is just one of any number of pseudonyms he uses, a character trait that is more than simply a ruse to keep the schizophrenia twist under wraps until the final reel. In having no identity, 'Jack' becomes emblematic of his times. His apartment is homogenized by generic products. He is just another suit and tie at the office, a stooge for the company when he's out on the road. The film establishes its cynical credentials with the nature of his work: 'Jack' analyzes car wrecks to determine whether his firm should instigate a recall of one of their models because of a technical fault, the bottom line being, does a recall cost more than an out-of-court settlement? The constant travelling leaves 'Jack' prone to insomnia. He lies awake fretting about his material possessions. He is the middle-class consumer personified. He is everything the film rails against.

Initially, he finds comfort in attending support groups for the terminally ill; it allows him a pretence at emotionalism in a lifestyle that is otherwise sterile. Then, when a chance encounter, followed shortly by the 'accidental' destruction of his condo in an explosion, leads to him sharing a dilapidated old house with Tyler, he discovers a cathartic release in bare-knuckle fighting. Tyler is the voice of 'Jack's disaffection ('we're a generation of men raised by women,' he says at one point, 'and I'm wondering if another woman is really the answer we need'), goading him into an escalating series of violent acts.

The brawling starts in the car park outside Tyler's local bar. The regulars get interested. The venue shifts to the basement. They get organized. 'We were finding something out,' 'Jack' muses. And what they find out is this: that with every blow thrown or taken, with every fight won or lost, they are re-asserting their masculinity, as well as reacting against socially accepted values such as career, consumerism and marriage. At the inaugural meeting of Fight Club, a close-up shows one of the combatants removing his wedding ring. A businessman who asks to fight is instructed by Tyler to 'lose the tie'. The trappings of normalcy are stripped away: 'Jack' stops wearing a tie to the office, sporting bruises in lieu; at a high-level meeting, he bares teeth that are caked in blood. His rejection of the workplace comes to a head when he beats himself up in front of his supervisor in order to blackmail him into a lucrative severance deal. (This aspect of fighting – self-immolation – is revisited when Tyler orders Fight Club members to instigate a fight with a complete stranger … and lose. One Fight Clubber manages to provoke a priest into taking a swing at him.)

The self-contained violence of *Fight Club* – which is brutal enough as it is: fists connect with faces; body blows are hammered home; heads smack against the concrete floor - spills out into society as Tyler encourages his acolytes towards anarchy. They commit violence against property: expensive cars, office buildings, franchise outlets (coffee shops, car dealerships, computer retailers) and pieces of corporate art are vandalized. Soap and other household products are used to manufacture explosives. Project Mayhem – such is Tyler's revolutionist re-invention of Fight Club called – culminates in an act of terrorism: a plot to destroy the headquarters of America's financial institutions. The intended result: to free society from consumerism; to create complete equality.

A similar aim drives John Doe (Kevin Spacey), the most cerebral serial killer this side of a certain Dr Lecter, in Fincher's earlier film, **Seven** (1995): to send a wake-up call to a society too self-obsessed to recognize the urban horrors which permeate it. Basing his modus operandi on the seven deadly sins, he stages murder as metaphor: a grotesquely obese man tied up and made to eat until his stomach bursts (Gluttony); a pederast and wastrel tied to a bed, deliberately kept alive for a year while his muscles atrophy, his body becomes covered in bed sores and malnutrition sets in (Sloth); a frequenter of prostitutes compelled at gunpoint to strap on a knife-like dildo and engage in intercourse with a hooker (Lust); a narcissistic fashion model inflicted with injuries to her face, a mobile phone glued to one hand, a bottle of sleeping pills to the other, giving her a choice of suicide or life at the cost of disfigurement (Pride). There is a literary antecedent in the lawyer (Greed) forced to sever a pound of his own flesh (Shakespeare, *The Merchant of Venice*).

Of the two detectives working the case, the soon-to-retire William Somerset (Morgan Freeman) and the impulsive and temperamental David Mills (Brad Pitt), it is Somerset who twigs early on to John Doe's twisted homage to the classics. In a scene that says a lot about the kind of intellectual non-comprehension John Doe, in his own sociopathic way, is taking action against, Somerset visits a library after closing time, allowed admittance by a friend who works there as a security guard. As Somerset walks among rows of books, selecting works by Dante and Chaucer, the security staff sit above the study area, engrossed in a hand of poker. 'I'll never understand,' he berates them, 'all these books, a world of knowledge at your fingertips, and what do you do? You play poker all night.'

Somerset, ostensibly, is the most sympathetic character, softly spoken and rational. He is continually contrasted with Mills, who is edgy and hot-headed. Yet Somerset is wound tighter than a watch spring. He has no friends on the force. His home life is empty. He sets a metronome ticking as he lies in bed; later, unable to sleep, he throws a flick-knife at a dartboard. For all his intellectualism, his humanity is in danger of ebbing to glum cynicism. At the end of the film, he quotes Hemingway – 'the world is a fine place and worth fighting for', then adds, 'I agree with the second part'.

The darkness of *Seven*'s worldview (all but the last 20 minutes are played out in a shadowy and rain-swept city where the sky is hardly ever glimpsed) is compounded in its shattering conclusion. John Doe, jealous of Mills's attractive young wife (Gwyneth Paltrow), taunts him with an account of how he killed her, goading him to an act of homicide. Thus, in his own death, John Doe completes the cycle, casting himself as Envy and Mills as Wrath. And through this diabolical finale, Somerset is impotent, pleading with Mills – to no avail – not to kill a man who has rejected every tenet of life.

Seven's nihilism, like *Fight Club*'s, stems from a fusion of urban disaffection and millennial angst. Likewise *Strange Days*: the city as purgatory, the new millennium ushered in by violence and paranoia. But the roots of these dark visions lead back to post-war Britain. **Brighton Rock** (John Boulting, 1947) is in fact set between the two world wars, something made clear in an opening credits disclaimer that takes pains to point out that such a Brighton no longer exists. The narrative begins with the revenge killing of journalist Fred Hale (Alan Wheatley) by youthful gang leader Pinkie Brown (Richard Attenborough), who goes on to silence witnesses, either by courtship and marriage in the case of naive young waitress Rose (Carol Marsh), or by killing one of his own, Spicer (Wylie Watson), advancing on him until he plunges through a broken balustrade and falls to his death. At the same time, he struggles to defend his protection rackets from heavyweight mobster Colleoni (Charles Goldner).

Brighton Rock paints its resort town setting as a seedy, violent place, the tourist-thronged seafront merely a façade. Leisure activities disguise criminal operations: it is from the ghost train that Pinkie despatches Hale into the roiling waters beneath the pier; at the racecourse he betrays another of his own, leaving the man to a group of Colleoni's razor-wielding thugs. His treachery is rewarded when Colleoni's men then go after Pinkie himself, leaving him scarred and badly bleeding.

The film's violence is shocking as much for Pinkie's detachment – there is an utter lack of emotion in Attenborough's performance – as his youth. In an early scene, he tells Rose that he's seventeen; indeed, his face is smooth and unwhiskered. The expression 'baby-faced' (with its inevitable correlation with American gangster George Nelson) comes to mind. Incidental details emphasize the point: he doesn't drink or smoke (i.e. he's underage); he wins a doll at a shooting range, which he later destroys in a fit of pique. And like a child who has been left undisciplined and given no moral instruction, he has no concept of accountability or the value of human life. As the net closes towards the end of the film, he tries to persuade Rose – the girl he doesn't love, and whose love for him he denigrates (out of earshot he calls her 'a right slut') – to join him in a suicide pact. A pact he has every intention of surviving. But when Rose, terrified by the religious implications of his request ('it's a mortal sin'), throws away the gun he has pressed into her hands, he is left defenceless and terrified. In a brilliantly Faustian moment, with arrest imminent and nowhere to run, he falls from the pier into the same waters that claimed Hale's life.

Brighton Rock, for all that many of its external scenes take place in bright sunlight against a backdrop of deckchairs and ice-cream stands, is pure film noir. The religious elements of Graham Greene's original novel (Greene co-wrote the screenplay with Terence Rattigan) may be present in the film's symbolism (when Spicer falls to his death, he dislodges a gas pipe that sends a Hadean gout of flame jetting out), but there is no doubt that first and foremost *Brighton Rock* is a gangster film – it was released in America as *Young Scarface* – with a cruel, amoral and ultimately cowardly protagonist, a man who scorns and fears love and intimacy; a man who, in the final analysis, believes in nothing.

Pinkie's heir apparent appeared three years later in the form of Tom Riley (Dirk Bogarde) in **The Blue Lamp** (Basil Dearden, 1950). The film is a departure from *Brighton Rock* in several ways: it relocates the action from a resort town to the heart of the metropolis, London; it replaces the straight-razor

'I'll drop you': the villain prominent in poster artwork for *The Blue Lamp*

with a pistol; and its sacrificial victim is not a shabby journalist but upstanding police constable George Dixon (Jack Warner).

The Blue Lamp is often cited for one of two reasons: launching the spin-off series *Dixon of Dock Green* (never mind that the character dies in the film), and being the first mainstream British production to use the word 'bastard' (a sergeant's exhortation to a canteen full of constables as they are called away from their cuppa: 'they're on to the bastard that shot George Dixon'). This thematic disparity characterizes the film: the rose-tinted portrayal of friendly bobbies on the beat sits cheek by jowl with the snivelling nastiness of its villain. In an early scene, Riley laughingly terrifies his girlfriend by pointing the gun at her; later, concerned about ensuring her silence, he attempts to strangle her. Riley commits two robberies – at a jewellery store and a cinema – coshing a police constable as he makes his escape from the former, and a doorman for no other reason than he's there at the latter.

Scenes of light-hearted banter between Dixon and his wife find their contrast in the film noir visuals that characterize Riley's nocturnal knavery. Likewise, Dixon's fellow constables, who cheerfully rehearse their male voice choir early in the film, are replaced by a group of grim-faced, vengeful policemen converging on Riley at the climax, having pursued him to a White City Stadium dog race after his girlfriend informs on him over Dixon's murder. Here, the imagery is more in keeping with a western, the officers advancing implacably like gunslingers.

Dixon would go on to earn a place in the hearts of a generation, a pillar of moral rectitude, courtesy of the series. His demise in the film, though, is as unheroic and pointless as it gets. He happens upon Riley, roll-neck sweater pulled up to disguise his face, about to make a run for it having robbed a cinema box office. Riley's eyes are dilated with fear as Dixon advances on him:

> **Riley:** Get back.
> **Dixon:** Drop that and don't be a fool. Drop it, I say.
> **Riley:** I'll drop you. [Dixon advances.] Get back. This
> thing works. Get back! [He fires two shots and Dixon falls.]

Post-war hardship resulted in the depiction of the criminal element, in many films of the time, as spivs or black-marketeers. In *Brighton Rock* and *The Blue Lamp* a new type of social deviant emerged: the juvenile delinquent. Notwithstanding that Attenborough and Bogarde were respectively 24 and 30 when they played Pinkie and Riley (older than the teenage-based social grouping by which we understand the term 'juvenile delinquent' today), the emphasis is on the youthfulness of their characters as the defining aspect of their vicious behaviour. They are from destitute backgrounds; products, it can be argued, of their environment. 'Restless and ill-adjusted youngsters,' as *The Blue Lamp*'s voice-over narrative calls them, made this way because of 'the effects of a childhood spent in homes broken and demoralized by the war.'

In Elia Kazan's **On the Waterfront** (1954) there is also an analogue between an economically depressed, working class environment and the protagonists' capacity for violence. Marlon Brando plays Terry Malloy, a one-time boxer whose title hopes have been frittered away throwing fights on behalf of corrupt union boss Johnny Friendly (Lee J Cobb), now paid off with a cushy non-job on the docks. His brother, Charlie (Rod Steiger), is well established in the hierarchy of Johnny's staff. Terry's fellow longshoremen have it significantly less easy: obtaining work on a daily basis is dependent upon payment of one's dues to Johnny. Crime investigations are probing the union's dealings[10] and anyone cooperating is likely to end up dead.

Character motivations are overshadowed by the knowledge that both Kazan and screenwriter Budd Schulberg named names at the McCarthy hearings – the film often seems like a justification for 'ratting' – but, ostensibly, Terry's social conscience is pricked by the rhetoric of a crusading priest (Karl Malden) and his feelings for Edie (Eva Marie Saint), the sister of Johnny's latest murder victim. He struggles with the dilemma of whether or not to testify in court. Through Charlie, Johnny offers him an even more profitable job (all he has to do, in waterfront parlance, is keep 'D&D' – deaf and dumb). When Terry refuses the offer, in a justifiably classic scene, a deeper sense of resentment comes to the fore:

> **Terry:** It was you, Charlie… . That night at the Garden, you came into my dressing room and said, 'Kid, it ain't your night. We're going for the price on Wilson.' It ain't your night! … So what happens? This bum Wilson, he gets the title shot, outdoors in the ball park. And what do I get? A one-way ticket to Palookaville. It was you, Charlie. You was my brother. You shoulda looked out for me …
> **Charlie:** I always had a bet down for you. You saw some money.
> **Terry:** See! You don't understand. I coulda had class, I coulda been a contender. I coulda been somebody, instead of being a bum, which is what I am.

The violence here is that done to Terry's hopes and aspirations – a violence done by his own brother. The violence soon becomes physical: Charlie is killed by Johnny for being unable to guarantee Terry's continued silence; there is an attack on Terry's life as he and Edie are nearly mown down by a truck; going back to the waterfront after his testimony, he is badly beaten, Johnny's men interceding when Terry almost betters their boss in a hitherto straight fight. Finally, barely able to stand, the onus is placed on him to walk into the warehouse and lead the longshoremen (none of whom intervene during the beating) back to work, symbolically breaking Johnny's power over the union.

With its authentically grimy docks and dull tenement interiors, *On the Waterfront* establishes an effective sense of place. Violence is perpetrated using fist, gun or baseball bat; Charlie is hung up on a grappling hook after he is killed. There is nothing heroic or exciting about it. An anti-violence sentiment is clear when Johnny's thugs attack the church where the priest is encouraging the longshoremen to air their grievances.

This is a bleak film and, in its ceaseless efforts to sanctify the informer, sometimes tiresome, but important in its correlation of violence and environment. Its depiction of joyless working conditions and the exploitation of a social underclass make it very much a precursor of Seventies cinema. In **Taxi Driver** (Scorsese, 1976), the socially dysfunctional Travis Bickle (de Niro) takes a job

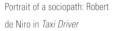

Portrait of a sociopath: Robert de Niro in *Taxi Driver*

driving a cab so that he can work nights (like 'Jack' in *Fight Club*, he suffers from insomnia). A Vietnam veteran, he is plagued by 'bad ideas' and is unable to find peace of mind from the sewer of humanity as represented by nocturnal New York. 'Each time I returned the cab to the garage,' he muses, early in the film, 'I had to clean the come off the back seat. Some nights I'd clean off the blood.'

He becomes smitten with the politically motivated Betsy (Cybill Shepherd), an idealist who campaigns for presidential candidate Charles Pallantine (Leonard Harris). 'She appeared like an angel out of this filthy mess,' is how he describes her, evidence that his perceptions are hardly objective. He tentatively instigates a relationship with her, but when his social abilities prove inadequate, her (understandable) rejection of him pushes him over the edge. He buys a veritable arsenal of guns, equips himself with a combat knife, works out obsessively and plans an assassination attempt on Pallantine. When this is foiled, he develops another strange relationship with an unattainable female figure, this time underage prostitute Iris (Jodie Foster)[11]. Driven to a final act of violence by the pimp (Harvey Keitel) who exploits her, Bickle commits three murders: pimp, john, and the proprietor of the rooming house to which Iris takes her clients. He is left badly wounded. Slumping down near the sobbing Iris, he turns no less than two guns on himself – both are empty. As police officers swarm into the blood-spattered room, he lifts a hand, blood dripping to the floor, and makes a gun with his fingers which he points at his head. There is something in the act that is both childlike and utterly final.

But he does not die. In a coda as ambiguous as it is unexpected, he survives and is declared a hero. A pan across the wall of his apartment takes in any number of press clippings praising him for his vigilante actions. Pinned next to them is a letter, ostensibly from Iris's parents, with whom she has been reunited, and who venerate him for her return. He returns to driving a cab. However, his colleagues make no mention of his actions, there seems to have been no legal repercussions for what (notwithstanding the unsavoury practises of the victims) remains a triple homicide and the handwriting of Betsy's parents letter bears a remarkable similarity to that in Bickle's own journal entries. (The theory that his 'hero' status is merely fantasy invites further comparison with 'Jack' in *Fight Club*: how much of the film actually occurs in its anti-hero's mind? Viewed on this level, Bickle is even more emblematic of the impotent rage many of us feel towards society at times but never physically act upon.)

However one interprets *Taxi Driver*, Travis Bickle is truly a tragic character. He enters the film alienated and in search of something. He is misguided enough to take a job that thrusts him into the fetid heart of a city that has already sickened him. In a key scene, fellow cabbie Wizard (Peter Boyle) tries to offer him a few words of advice: 'A man takes a job and that job, well it becomes what he is. You do a thing and that's what you are.' Which summarizes Bickle's dichotomy: he drives a cab to fill up the empty, lonely insomniac hours, but in doing so is witness first-hand to the social horrors that poison his mind.

Taxi Driver remains one of the few films that intelligently analyze the mindset of the vigilante. Mostly, films that tread this path err towards exploitation. Michael Winner's **Death Wish** (1974) is a case in point. The plot is basic: following an attack that leaves his wife dead and his daughter traumatized, mild-mannered architect Paul Kersey (Charles Bronson) takes the law into his own hands when the police prove ineffectual. His cathartic spree begins when a client insists on talking business at his gun club, encouraging Kersey to take a few pot shots at paper targets. Kersey turns out to be very adept at marksmanship, and when the client gives him a revolver, he quickly graduates from a shooting range to the streets of New York, from paper targets to people. The second half of the film is devoted to Kersey wandering the city's less salubrious areas, luring muggers and delinquents into attempted attacks, whereupon he summarily dispatches them.

Eventually, Kersey becomes a hero of sorts. Even the police, when they catch up with him, seem to sanction his behaviour. Instead of prosecuting him for what, at the very least, amounts to manslaughter, they cut him a deal whereby his relocation from New York is rewarded by their turning a blind eye. The film ends with Kersey arriving in another city – Chicago – and eyeing up a couple of street punks, ready to dispense a little more wild justice.

While the essence of the narrative (or at least the horrific crime that sets the narrative in motion) holds a modicum of social resonance, its execution and reliance on stereotypes – not to mention its refusal to consider the dehumanizing effects of its protagonist's actions – mark it out as a hymn to gung-ho, right-wing gun-owners. Like Ferrera's *Ms .45*[12], which delivers a similar plot, but with a supposedly 'feminist' spin in that it is the victimized woman herself who turns vigilante, a very real social issue is bastardized into a series of vengeful, gun-toting set pieces.

Nonetheless, the influence of *Death Wish* is still visible, two decades on, in Joel Schumacher's **Falling Down** (1992), a film which points towards *Seven* and *Fight Club* in blaming its anti-hero's actions on the desensitizing effects of urban life. It begins with a scene of road-rage – or rather traffic-jam-rage, since it's rush hour and the tailback is interminable. D-Fens (Michael Douglas), so called after his personalized licence plate, grows increasingly agitated by the melange of blaring horns, glaring orange lights of the advanced direction signs, and shrieks emanating from the school bus in the next lane. He abandons his car and starts walking across the city. 'I'm going home,' he offers, by way of explanation.

The city is sweltering in a heat wave. Everyone is on a short fuse. D-Fens's odyssey takes the form of a series of confrontations. The first is with a Korean shopkeeper who charges him an extortionate price for a can of Coke. An argument develops and the shopkeeper reaches under the counter for a baseball bat. D-Fens wrestles it from him and, in a borderline xenophobic scene, berates the man as much for his pidgin English as for his steep prices. D-Fens's use of violence begins

D-Fens (Michael Douglas) turns against his wife (Barbara Herschey) in *Falling Down*

here: violence against property as he uses the baseball bat to wreak havoc on the shop.

It isn't long before he uses it on people. Crossing a wasteground he is approached by a couple of youths – gang members – who demand money from him. One produces a flick-knife. D-Fens lays him out with the baseball bat, chases the other off, then pockets the blade. Again, as he disarms others, he arms himself.

Their paths cross again when they attempt a drive-by on D-Fens. Fortunately for him, they seem to be the most incompetent gang in the hood: they kill a few innocent passers-by, miss D-Fens entirely, then crash their car. D-Fens calmly walks over and avails himself of their bag of guns. At this point, he hasn't crossed the line by killing anyone – his next encounter sees him discharge his weapon into the ceiling of a burger bar when he is treated offhandedly by the staff (pure wish-fulfilment for any audience member who has received second-rate service at a fast-food franchise) – but that changes when he evades police by sheltering in an army surplus clothing store owned by a deranged neo-Nazi (Frederic Forrest). A right-wing homophobe who collects war memorabilia, he initially sees D-Fens as a kindred spirit and offers him a rocket launcher. When D-Fens protests, the store owner attacks him, threatening him at gunpoint. D-Fens stabs and disarms him, then shoots him repeatedly. Then he leaves, with the rocket launcher.

From here on in, his use of force, while still firmly grounded in social protest, takes on a darker aspect. He opens up with the rocket launcher at a construction site, objecting to the works as an example of local government mis-spending. Raving against class, elitism and the idle rich as he trespasses on a members-only golf course, he terrifies someone into a heart attack. When he finally arrives back 'home', it is with threatening intentions towards his estranged wife and daughter.

Motivated throughout by the awfulness of modern life – most of his misadventures are simply negative reactions to insalubrious situations – his final act is one of ultimate rejection, not dissimilar to Mr Blue's in *The Taking of Pelham 123*. In a stand-off with Prendergast (Robert Duvall), the detective investigating the trail of mayhem D-Fens has left behind him, he provokes his own death by reaching for a weapon. Prendergast shoots and kills him. Like Kitano in *Battle Royale*, his gun turns out to be a toy; he orchestrates his own death with a water-pistol. And like Pinkie in *Brighton Rock*, he plunges from the end of a pier, his death the inevitable price for his rejection of social conventions.

censorship and controversy

When the killer is unmasked at the end of **Scream 2** (Wes Craven, 1998), the legal repercussions of his crimes don't seem to worry him. In fact, it is quite the opposite: he is positively looking forward to his day in court. 'I've got my whole defence planned out,' he sneers. 'I'm going to blame the movies ... . This [the spate of murders] was just a prelude to the trial. These days it's all about the trial. The effects of cinema violence on society. I'll get Cochran to represent me. Bob Dole on the witness stand in my defence. Hell, the Christian Coalition'll pay my legal fees.'

It's a pertinent point. The 'Scream' trilogy has satirized every element of the horror film from its 'rules' and iconography to the diminishing returns of its inevitable sequels. Here, Craven and screenwriter Kevin Williamson take a swipe at the supposed effects of violent movies. But, as the scene demonstrates, blaming cinema is usually the smokescreen for an ulterior motive.

As the sensationalism over O J Simpson proved, trials often become media events (hence the reference to Johnny Cochran, Simpson's defence counsel, in the above quoted scene) and can be valuable in terms of publicity, and by extension career progression, to those either involved in the legal process, or the media pundits who pontificate on the proceedings.

When films are cited in trials, it is normally during mitigation. Mitigation occurs when a case is unwinnable and the defence bargain for as low a sentence as possible, enumerating whatever factors might be relevant (or might be perceived to be relevant) to the defendant's actions. Hence the tendency, eagerly seized on by the tabloid press, to shift accountability from the actual perpetrator, and find something else on which to pin the blame.

Cinema as scapegoat

On 19 August 1987, Michael Ryan armed himself with a 9mm Beretta and a semi-automatic rifle, and drove from his home town of Hungerford, in England, to Savernake Forest. Here he shot and killed mother-of-two Sue Godfrey who was picnicking with her children. Leaving the children physically unharmed, but deeply traumatized, he drove to a nearby petrol station, refuelled his car and filled a spare container with petrol, which he later used to burn down his house. The petrol station attendant escaped death when Ryan's gun misfired. Ryan left hurriedly and returned to Hungerford.

Having retrieved a collection of survivalist gear he kept at home (Ryan was obsessed with military techniques and equipment), he burned down his house, killed his mother (with whom he lived) and his neighbours. Abandoning his car, he walked around Hungerford, eventually ending up at his old school. En route, he shot everyone he encountered. By the time police surrounded him in the school building, he had murdered 16 people. When they attempted to negotiate with him, he turned the gun on himself.

Because Michael Ryan is dead, he will never be able to account for his actions. He was a loner, which, in itself, is not necessarily synonymous with sociopathic tendencies. He was, however, socially inadequate: that he still resided with his mother indicates a lack of contact with, or an inability to function in, the outside world. His primary interests were guns, survivalism and combat gear – all the trappings and iconography of militarism.

The tabloid press, however, were quick to assign the blame. They linked two tenuous facts – that Ryan owned a VCR and that the then most popular title at a local video hire shop was First Blood (Ted Kotcheff, 1982) – and whipped up a campaign of scaremongering and hyperbole so effective that, 15 years later, the name

Sylvester Stallone as Rambo in the much-maligned *First Blood*

of the leading character, Rambo, still features in newspaper headlines every time a sociopath, through no other reason than their own psychological defects, commits an act of violence[1].

In looking for someone or something to blame, the media overlooked two prime candidates: the Wiltshire Shooting Centre, who supplied him with weaponry and ammunition and, crucially, Ryan himself. Ultimately, it was he who decided to kill, and did so of his own volition. Nonetheless, as a result of media hysteria – UK tabloids *The Sun*, *The Star*, the *Daily Mail* and *The Mirror* all ran headlines which treated the name Rambo almost as an adjective – the film, which had been screened on BBC1 a year before the incident, disappeared from British television for a decade. The BBC opted not to show it again.

It has since been screened twice (at the time of writing) on Channel 5, and is available on home video, certificated 15; it remains a gripping, if occasionally badly acted, film which has something definite to say about prejudice and the aftermath of violence (see chapter five for a fuller discussion).

But the tabloid press have never allowed the merits of a film to detract from its suitability in the witch-hunt stakes. Oliver Stone's **Natural Born Killers** (1994) – the very point of which is to question the media's obsession with making celebrities out of psychopaths – was singled out when, between 7 and 8 March 1995, teenage couple Ben Darras and Sarah Edmondson shot two people, killing one and seriously wounding the other, as they drove across America. Six months earlier, Florence Rey and Audry Maupin had notched up four fatal shootings during a running gun battle with police in Paris. In both cases, the only similarity between actual events and Stone's film was that the perpetrators were a romantically involved couple. Ergo, the headlines could just as easily (and just as arbitrarily) have picked up on *Bonnie and Clyde*, *Badlands*, *Wild at Heart* or *True Romance*.

Natural Born Killers was always going to be controversial, though. Based on an original screenplay by Quentin Tarantino, who publicly denounced Stone for the liberties he took with it, the film opened in America after much wrangling between the filmmakers and the MPAA (Motion Picture Association of America) over the amount of cuts required to lower the rating from NC-17 to R[2]. That was in

Social deviant: Woody Harrelson in *Natural Born Killers*

August 1994. As a result of the adverse publicity, its release in Britain was delayed. Scheduled for release on 18 November 1994, it was put on hold by the BBFC (British Board of Film Classification) pending high-level discussions about its certification. Rehashing second-hand hyperbole from the American press, some British tabloids called for the film to be banned, while others erroneously reported that it had. (This despite a statement issued by then BBFC director James Ferman that it had not been banned, but was merely under consideration[3].) *Natural Born Killers* was eventually granted a UK cinema release, certificated 18, on 24 February 1995. Predictably, the video release engendered another storm in a teacup (as did that of *Reservoir Dogs*, which enjoyed extended cinema bookings as debate raged on whether it would be certificated for video).

Of course, a film doesn't have to be cited in a criminal case in order for the press to call for its suppression. David Cronenberg's **Crash** (1996) opened in British cinemas on a wave of censure: there had been angry walkouts at the Cannes film festival; Westminster City Council had banned it outright; then Heritage Secretary Virginia Bottomley had called for it to be banned UK-wide (although she hadn't even seen the film at that point). Its subject matter meant that misunderstanding and outraged moralizing were inevitable. An adaptation of J G Ballard's novel, it portrays a society so desensitized that bored professional couple James and Catherine Ballard (James Spader and Deborah Kara Unger) can only achieve sexual arousal through car wrecks. This element of their relationship brings them into contact with Vaughan (Elias Koteas), a bisexual

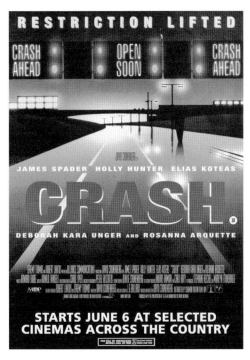

Advertising for *Crash*, wittily playing on its delayed release

whose tastes are even more deviant: he devotes his time to staging life-threatening re-enactments of notorious car crashes, including those that claimed the lives of James Dean and Jayne Mansfield.

More violence is done to machine than to man during the course of the film, but the sexual scenes are graphic, loveless and have about them a brutality that makes the buckled metal and gashed paintwork of the wrecks seem joyful by comparison. As with much of his work, Cronenberg evinces little emotional involvement with his characters. He seems content to stand back and observe them, refusing even to draw a conclusion. He leaves the final word to his audience. Sadly, tabloid efforts to pre-empt the opinions of his potential audience not only saddled the film with negative expectations, but also almost kept it from British screens. Its original January 1997 release date delayed, *Crash* was released in UK cinemas in June of that year and on rental video in June 1998. Appearance of a film on rental video is usually a matter of months (*Pulp Fiction* was still playing at many cinemas when it reached the shelves of video stores). Advertising for *Crash*'s video release wittily announced 'restriction lifted'.

Abel Ferrara's acclaimed **Bad Lieutenant** (1992) also suffered a delay before appearing on video – two years in this case, and even then only after it was trimmed by three minutes. Controversy, though, was always guaranteed. Ferrara's vision of a man descending into a paranoid madness of his own creation contains scenes that are as graphic and challenging as anything in *The Driller Killer* and *Ms .45*. The titular corrupt police officer (Harvey Keitel) – he is referred to in the credits only as 'the lieutenant' – is a drunkard and a drug-user; he has gambling debts that are out of control; his use of violence is dictated by mood; he abuses his authority (in one particularly excruciating scene, he makes a couple of teenage girls caught driving without a licence expose themselves and simulate an act of fellatio while he masturbates). Assigned to investigate the rape of a nun, he is overwhelmed with Catholic guilt. Unable to comprehend how the nun can forgive the men who violated her, he hallucinates a vision of Christ, during which he verbally abuses Him. Yet the film ends with the lieutenant affecting an act of forgiveness, almost as if pleading for his own salvation. Redemption comes too late, however, and he is gunned down by the bookies to whom his debts have become unpayable.

As with *Crash*, as with any number of other films that the tabloid press have called to be banned, no real-life cases were allayed with *Bad Lieutenant*. It was simply seized upon by scare-mongers and tarred with the brush of assumptions about its director's reputation.

Arguably the most insensitive example of tabloid behaviour – and certainly the most spurious citing of a film as scapegoat – was the heart-breaking James Bulger case. The facts, although they defy belief, were simple: on 12 February 1993, the two-year-old was led away from a crowded shopping centre by Robert Thompson and Jon Venables. Evidence indicates they interfered with him. They took him to a canal where they intended to drown him. When this failed, they dragged him to a railway line. They poured paint on him and used bricks to beat him to death.

Thompson and Venables were ten years old.

Infanticide is a heinous act; difficult to comprehend, impossible to understand. When committed by adults, as in the case of Moors murderers Ian Brady and Myra Hindley who assaulted and killed three children between 1963 and 1965, objective reporting is hard: the only adjective that fits the bill is 'evil'. But when the perpetrators are children, it puts a very different spin on things. An already distressing subject is made even thornier. A clear rationale needs to be established, and as such should have been along these lines: at ten, a child is old enough to know the difference between right and wrong.

Sadly, the tabloid press were not clear-sighted enough to maintain focus. Instead of assigning responsibility to Thompson and Venables, or considering the role of their parents in their upbringing, they went looking for a scapegoat. They found it in the low-budget and forgettable horror sequel **Child's Play 3** (Jack Bender, 1991). The villain of this franchise – which reached a fourth instalment in 1999 with the critically well-received *Bride of Chucky* – is a doll (voiced by Brad Dourif), possessed by the spirit of a serial killer, who wreaks havoc in a variety of murderous set-pieces. In the third film, set in a military college, there are scenes involving a ghost train and Chucky being splattered by a paintball gun. The use of paint and the railway line locale were the basis of the correlation the media drew between the film and James Bulger's death. As David Kerekes and David Slater point out in *See No Evil*, 'So ambiguous are the supposed links that if we were to transpose *Child's Play 3* with *Home Alone 2* the results would be just the same – indeed, the latter film would be more fitting as it features a child being separated from his parents and terrorized by two older males.'[4] Moreover, when police searched Thompson and Venables' houses, they did not find among the respective video collections copies of *Child's Play 3*. Thus the denunciation of the film smacks, at best, of self-serving moral crusading, unfounded on fact. What is worse – and a damning indictment of the media's motivations – is that, during these spurious 'comparisons' to the film, the character of Chucky was treated as a stand-in for James Bulger. While the comparison between Darras/Edmondson or Rey/Maupin and *Natural Born Killers* equated actual homicidal lovers with a fictitious couple, the James Bulger/*Child's Play 3* furore equated a real-life victim with a cinematic villain. How much additional and uncalled-for heartache this type of 'reporting' must have caused James's parents can only be guessed at.

Withdrawal: the self-imposed ban

Stanley Kubrick's **A Clockwork Orange** (1971) was a controversy waiting to happen. The source novel, by Anthony Burgess, was a response to an attack on Burgess's first wife by a group of AWOL American soldiers in 1944. He explored his fears of a society desensitized by violence using a highly stylized language, which he called Nadsat (a mixture of colloquial Russian and Cockney rhyming slang). Burgess intended that the language of the novel would act as a barrier between the reader and the acts being described on the page.

Even though Kubrick retained the argot of Nadsat for the dialogue (preserving such lines as 'getting ready to do the old in-out-in-out on a weepy young devotchka' and 'viddy well, little brother, viddy well'), a film is more immediate than a novel. The reign of sadistic, thrill-seeking violence inflicted by Alex (Malcolm McDowell) and his 'droogs' (gang members) made the transfer to the screen with visceral intensity. Burgess's literary stylizations found their visual equivalent in Kubrick's

Dark iconography: Malcolm McDowell in *A Clockwork Orange*

technically adroit direction; but on film, such stylizations only enhance iconography.

A Clockwork Orange is very much a film of two halves. It begins with Alex rampant, assaulting tramps, instigating fights with rival gangs (flick knives, bicycle chains and broken bottles are the weapons of choice), breaking and entering, raping and, finally, killing. (Sex and death are fused in the image of Alex bludgeoning a woman with a sculpture of a giant phallus.) Nor is he above doling out beatings to his droogs for questioning his leadership or mocking his love of Beethoven. His luck soon runs out, though. His gang, rebelling, leave him to face the police and a murder charge.

The remainder of the film charts society's revenge on him. Even before his conviction, he is beaten and spat on by the officers who interrogate him. Sent down, he survives in prison only by toadying to the chaplain; homosexual rape is a constant threat. He volunteers for a new psychological process, Ludovico's technique, designed to make the habitually violent recidivist recoil from the very thought of future offences. Alex undergoes further indignities during treatment, forcibly restrained, eyes pried open, scenes of violence projected interminably on a screen before him while his beloved Beethoven plays on the soundtrack. A side effect leaves him unable to listen to the Ninth Symphony.

Pronounced fit to rejoin society, he is *persona non grata* at the family home. Walking the streets, he is set upon by tramps, then picked up by two policemen (former droogs) who beat him and leave him for dead. Disorientated, he seeks assistance at the house of one of his earlier victims, a reactionary writer (Patrick Magee) who is critical of the government and their use of Ludovico's technique. Realizing who he is, the writer drugs him and imprisons him in an upstairs room. From the room below, he plays the Ninth at great volume, driving Alex to a suicide attempt by hurling himself from a window. Surviving, albeit hospitalized, the government weather the bad publicity by rescinding the treatment. Alex, bribed for his silence, fantasizes about violent sexual gratification as he listens to the Ode to Joy. 'I was cured all right,' he muses.

The film, then (shorn of Burgess's moralistic final chapter where Alex, regretful of his crimes, begins to mature), is perversely amoral. There is lawless violence and sanctioned violence and they are equally ugly. Violence is part of the human condition and there is no solution, no cure.

A Clockwork Orange opened in the UK in January 1972, just two months after *Straw Dogs* (which, as we have seen, postulates that sometimes violence cannot be avoided and has to be confronted). *Straw Dogs* had incited heated debate on movie violence; *A Clockwork Orange* rode to box office success on a wave of controversy that eclipsed even the outrage over Peckinpah's film. Youths took to wearing the trademark white boiler suits and black bowler hats

Stanley Kubrick directs Miriam Karling and Malcolm McDowell in *A Clockwork Orange*

sported by Alex and his droogs. The press latched onto two cases for which the term 'copycat' could have been invented. A young Dutch woman holidaying in England was raped by a gang of youths; they chorused 'Singing in the Rain' (which Alex croons during a scene of sexual assault) while they attacked her. A youth of 16 kicked a tramp to death; the media described him as being obsessed with *A Clockwork Orange*. (It later transpired that he was a fan of the book; the film being X rated, he was unable to get into any screening of it.)

Opposition to the film was fierce. By March 1972, there were calls for then BBFC head Stephen Murphy, who had passed it uncut, to resign. The Home Secretary demanded a private screening.

Yet the disappearance of *A Clockwork Orange* from British screens for nearly 30 years was not as a result of media or government action, but at the behest of its own director. In his exhaustive biography, Vincent LoBrutto states: 'In 1974, Stanley Kubrick, concerned about all the real-life violent acts attributed to viewings of *A Clockwork Orange*, pulled the film from distribution in England.'[5] The terms of the withdrawal, backed up by Warner Brothers' legal department, made it illegal to screen the film in the country of Kubrick's residence (Kubrick moved to England in the Sixties, where he remained until his death in 1999). John Baxter, in his biography, attributes Kubrick's decision to a threat made against the director's family while he was shooting his next film, *Barry Lyndon* (1975), in Ireland.

The decision was made with the minimum of fuss or publicity. Indeed, it did not come to public attention until 1979, when the National Film Theatre in London put together a Kubrick retrospective and found they were denied a print of *A Clockwork Orange*. Independent London cinema, the Scala showed it surreptitiously, but when they dared to advertise a screening, found themselves on the receiving end of legal action. Subsequently, the film was not shown again in Britain until March 2000, a year after Kubrick's death. It has since been released to video and DVD. A resurgence of youths dressed as droogs and a spate of copycat crimes have been notable only by their non-occurrence.

The 'video nasties' controversy

When the video recorder first began to emerge as a lifestyle commodity, the type of product available for home viewing was as limited as it was unregulated. Major film distribution companies, perhaps distrustful of this new medium and the effect it might have on cinema attendance, chose not to release the blockbusting mainstream successes whose rights they owned. Two decades later, this caution has been proved unfounded, with rental and sales of videos and DVDs a profitable follow-up to a theatrical release. In the late Seventies and early Eighties, however, the video viewer's choices were narrower: bland documentaries, Electric Blue-type 'adult' titles and dirt-cheap exploitation movies that had maybe played a few drive-in circuits in America but had certainly never seen the inside of a cinema. Low budget fare has, of course, always been a staple of film production. Only the name has changed. In the early days they were called 'quota quickies' (after the utilitarian, money-conscious approach studios had towards them); then 'B' movies; now they are known by the acronym DTV (direct-to-video).

The titles released by companies like Vampix, Intervision and Vipco filled a need in the market created by lack of other offerings. They were mostly gore-spattered Italian horror films, while independent American productions pretty much accounted for the rest of the market. The latter ranged from cult classics like **The Texas Chain Saw Massacre** (Tobe Hooper, 1974) and *The Evil Dead* (1982), Sam Raimi's blistering directorial debut, to works of woeful ineptitude and deplorable content: *The Toolbox Murders* (Dennis Donnelly, 1978), *Fight For Your Life* (Robert A Endelson, 1977), *Love Camp 7* (R L Frost, 1968). In each case, the title gives ample indication of content, as do the Italian opuses – *Cannibal Holocaust* (Ruggero Deodato, 1979), *Deep River Savages* (Umberto Lenzi, 1972), *Bay of Blood* (Mario Bava, 1971). Needless to say, they flourished during a period when video distribution wasn't hampered by certification.

Titles were often changed, either to facilitate re-release in different packaging or cash in on the success (or notoriety) of another film. Hence the aforementioned *Bay of Blood* also being known as *L'Antefatto* (the original Italian title, which translates as 'After the Fact'), *Blood Bath*, *Twitch of the Death Nerve*, *The Ecology of a Crime*, *Carnage*, *The Last House on the Left Part II* and *New House on the Left*, these last two alternatives wrongly implying that it is some kind of sequel to Wes Craven's 1972 debut, The Last House on the Left – made one year after Bava's film!

Such tacky (and exploitative) re-titling – not to mention an emphasis on violence for its own sake, much of it directed against women – was responsible in no small part for the ensuing controversy. Video sleeve artwork, often reproduced in tabloid and trade press advertising, was lurid and did little to help (although it is ironic that the tabloids played such a great part in facilitating the subsequent bans). The backlash against video product began in the early Eighties with groups such as the National Festival of Light, the Community Standards Association and, most vociferously, Mary Whitehouse's National Viewers and Listeners Association, who took against the nature and advertising of the films on offer and publicly decried them. In 1982, the Advertising Standards Authority backed up complaints about the marketing of films like *The Driller Killer* and *Cannibal Holocaust*. In the same year, the Department of Public Prosecutions brought successful actions against titles including the aforementioned *Driller Killer* and *I Spit on Your Grave*. Media coverage gathered speed. The expression 'video nasty' became common coinage. Two years later, the Video Recordings Act 1984 was passed, decreeing that videos would be subject to the same system of certification applied to cinema releases. It was an appropriately Orwellian year.

Even today, with bans on, for instance, *The Texas Chain Saw Massacre* and *I Spit on Your Grave* repealed, it is difficult to define what constitutes a 'video nasty'. A statement made in the House of Commons by the DPP in July 1984 cited 39 titles under the general heading 'horror' (see Appendix) and is probably the closest thing there is to an 'official' list, although local council bans and prosecutions earned numerous other films the sobriquet.

Ultimately, while their content is often deeply politically incorrect, and the debate over the social implications of violent movies deeply subjective, perhaps the most pertinent question *vis-à-vis* the so-called 'video nasties' is whether any of them have any lasting cinematic value. In some cases (see the discussion on *I Spit on Your Grave* in chapter two), the reaction, however draconian, is easy to understand. Mostly, these films are drab, shoddy affairs, which all too keenly demonstrate their limitations, not only in terms of budget, but also in quality (or lack of it) of script, acting and direction. There are exceptions, however. *The Texas Chain Saw Massacre* is a unique cinematic experience, by turns shocking, comedic, exploitative, poetic, risible and impressive. Few films, certainly, can engender such a range of conflicting responses within 85 minutes. It begins with brother and sister Sally and Franklin (Marilyn Burns and Paul A Partain) visiting a secluded cemetery where their grandparents are buried, out of concern that the graves may have been vandalized. They journey there in a van with a couple of friends. Along the way they pick up a hitch-hiker who works in a nearby cattle slaughterhouse. Gruesome shots of how cows become beefburgers are intercut with the hitcher flipping out and attacking Sally and her friends with a knife. They expel him from the van, suffering only minor wounding, but his act of violence is merely a prelude.

Arriving at the cemetery, they make the mistake of visiting the now abandoned farmhouse where Sally and Franklin's grandfather used to live. The neighbouring property turns out to be inhabited by a family of inbred psychotics, the most pro-active of whom is Leatherface (Gunnar Hansen), so called because of the crudely fashioned piece he wears as a mask. Leatherface has a predilection for the improper use of power tools and a questionable talent for fashioning interior decorations from the bones of his victims.

Based on the equally bizarre home life of Ed Gein (also the inspiration for Norman Bates in *Psycho*), the most disturbing scenes have an emphasis that is not on violence (there are only two onscreen deaths, neither of which involve the eponymous chain saw) but suggestiveness. When Sally pads through one of the rooms in the Leatherface household, weird bone sculptures and clumps of feathers everywhere, the effect is infinitely more unsettling than any amount of blood-letting. Likewise, Sally's capture: her escape is made possible only when Leatherface's geriatric father, charged with her killing, is unable to hold a hammer let alone strike her with it. His repeated dropping of the implement allows her the opportunity to flee. As grim as the scene is, it is also blackly comic.

Of Hooper's subsequent efforts, only *Poltergeist* (1982)[6] and the television adaptation of Stephen King's *Salem's Lot* have demonstrated any of the promise shown in *The Texas Chain Saw Massacre*. Two of his lesser productions, *Death Trap* (1976) and *The Funhouse* (1981) were frequently cited as 'video nasties'.

Wes Craven, on the other hand, has gone on to significantly better things. His intelligence, understanding of genre conventions and fierce criticism of violence even as he depicts its worst excesses is as evident in the visceral intensity of *The Hills Have Eyes* (1978) and the mainstream iconography of *A Nightmare on Elm Street* as it is in the ironic genre deconstructionism of the 'Scream' trilogy. All of these traits have their roots in **The Last House on the Left** (Craven, 1972). Transposing the basic plot of Ingmar Bergman's **The Virgin Spring** (1959) to contemporary America, Craven presents a grim sex crime, its aftermath and the act of revenge that ensues. He does so with such a lack of sensationalism that the film has an almost documentary feel to it. Explicit and unflinching it may be, but there is definitely nothing prurient in his direction.

Comparison with Bergman's film is inevitable. *The Virgin Spring* is set in medieval Sweden, based on a folk legend. It has an essentially simple narrative: a young girl, Karin, is raped and killed in the woods by three goatherds (one, no more than a boy, is guilty only by his silent presence throughout the attack); they later seek shelter at a farmstead owned by Karin's parents; their crime is discovered; her father exacts a brutal revenge. This narrative is layered with questions of guilt (Karin's jealous sister wills something bad to happen to her), religion (Karin's parents are, initially, the very definition of God-fearing; Karin herself is on her way to deliver candles to a church when she is waylaid) and redemption (Karin's father birches himself before killing her attackers; afterwards, he pledges to build a church on the site of her murder). With its period setting, an ending that hints at a reaffirmation of the divine, and the exquisite cinematography of Sven Nykvist continually establishing juxtapositions between light and dark, *The Virgin Spring* emerges almost as a fable, even if its two short, self-contained scenes of violence leave little to the imagination.

The Last House on the Left, however, leaves its viewers with nowhere to hide. Notwithstanding the tag-line on its poster ('keep repeating, it's only a movie … only a movie … only a movie'), there is nothing in the way of reassurance. Craven's dark vision ups the ante on Bergman's film: there are two girls, not one – Mari (Sandra Cassel) and Phyllis (Lucy Grantheim); they are on their way not to church but to a heavy metal concert; the goatherds are replaced by a gang who have just broken out of prison (their crimes include drug pushing, rape, paedophilia and murder), led by the unspeakable Krug (David Hess). The attack on the girls is sustained and often unwatchable.

The perpetrators fetch up at the home of Dr and Mrs Collingwood, Mari's parents. The couple in Bergman's film are deeply religious; the Collingwoods are liberals. As with *The Virgin Spring*, belief in justice and non-violence is swiftly abandoned when the truth is discovered. Two of the gang are dealt with by Mrs Collingwood: she castrates one, having lured him with the promise of sex, and slits the throat of the other. Krug himself is despatched with a chain saw by Dr Collingwood[7]. Like *Straw Dogs*, the ending forces the film's protagonists to come to terms with their own capability for violence, no matter the violation of their daughter and the sanctity of their home. They have become dehumanized. Their tormentors are dead, but they have lost every tenet of belief by which they defined their own lives.

The Last House on the Left is an endurance course of a movie: difficult to watch, impossible to forget, frustratingly flawed (the scenes that demonstrate the ineffectuality of the authorities are so overplayed they seem to have wandered in from a different film entirely), and thoroughly depressing in its depiction of violence. But in showing us such unrelenting violence, Craven's call for an end to it comes across all the more powerfully.

Changing times

When James Ferman relinquished his role of BBFC director in 1999, superseded by Robin Duval, a new, more liberal era of certification was ushered in. *The Exorcist*, certified in the UK for cinema screenings only, was granted an 18 certificate for video. *The Texas Chain Saw Massacre* and *The Driller Killer* reappeared, the former enjoying a cinema re-release before its video release. The Appendix indicates other titles, previously banned on video, which have received certification over the last few years.

The trend has continued for new releases on the big screen. Explicit sexual material has been passed uncut in films like *Romance* (Catherine Breillat, 1999), *Intimacy* (Patrice Chereau, 2001) and *The Piano Teacher* (Michael Haneke, 2001). Eclipsing all of these, not just in terms of controversy but also as a sheer sustained visceral attack on the sensibilities of the viewer, is Virginie Despentes and Coralie Trinh Thi's ***Baise-moi*** (2001). While it might not match the polemic of *Romance*, the social realism of *Intimacy* or the cold intellectualism of *The Piano Teacher*, its combination of amoral violence and hardcore sexual imagery (scenes of fellatio and penetration), as well as its gleeful assimilation of any number of exploitation clichés, renders it an uncomfortable and disturbing viewing experience.

The nominal heroines are Nadine (Karen Bach) and Manu (Raffaélla Anderson), both of whom have suffered sexual objectification. Nadine works as a hooker, slobbered over by a parade of unappealing men. Manu 'acts' in hardcore features[8]. Manu is subjected to a gruelling rape when she and a friend are abducted by a gang of thugs and driven to a deserted warehouse. Manu's friend is beaten for trying to resist. Manu, on the other hand, suffers her ordeal unresponsively. Later, however, further traumatized by the suicide of her brother, she avails herself of the pistol he took his life with and begins living her life on the knife edge.

Fate soon throws her together with Nadine, wandering the streets following an assault on her prim and proper middle-class housemate.

95

Together, they set off across France, leaving a welter of violence in their wake. Indicative of how dehumanized they have become because of their respective lifestyles, their acts of homicide are utterly random and undelineated by gender or societal conditioning. A woman is killed, purely for the acquisition of her cash card. A non-threatening man they pick up is disposed of for no greater crime than insisting on using a prophylactic (they mock him as a 'condom dickhead'), while – at the other end of the social spectrum – a well-connected drug dealer who openly admits how much he admires them is just as summarily executed.

Their odyssey sees them (despite the carnal misuses visited upon them) as much in search of sexual abandonment as violent catharsis. Again, ambivalence in their motive emphasizes the haphazardness of their behaviour: a young man Manu picks up in a pub, who takes her back to his place and provides the night of no-strings-attached sex she was looking for is allowed to live (she even thanks him as she takes her leave), while the patrons of a sex club (who are at least honest about their reasons for attendance) are massacred, the women gunned down as casually as the men. One luckless thrill-seeker is made, in a role-reversal of *Deliverance* that is as excruciating as it is daring, to get on his knees and snort like a pig before Manu rams the barrel of her pistol in his anus and pulls the trigger.

Deliverance isn't the only film to which *Baise-moi* refers. There are also nods towards *Ms. 45* (Abel Ferrera, 1980) and *Thelma and Louise* (Ridley Scott, 1991), as well as to Tarantino and his imitators (in a rare scene of quiet contemplation, Nadine and Manu opine that their dialogue just isn't cool enough). Not that these pointers saved it from being banned by any number of local authority rulings in France. In Canada, it was banned outright. Ironically, it was the British censors who treated the film most liberally, prompting critics to speculate that if it hadn't been foreign and subtitled, it would never have been certificated.

As always with a film that incites such strong reaction, it is easy to get caught up in the controversy and overlook its aesthetic achievements. *Baise-moi*, however, offers little in the way of aesthetics. It is notable mainly for its visceral energy and the incessant assault it stages on the sensibilities of its audience. Indeed, it's tempting to ask what the point of *Baise-moi* is exactly. But, as Manu says early in the film: 'We'll follow our star and let rip the motherfucker side of our soul.' This one line of dialogue encapsulates the film perfectly: it's nihilistic, certainly, but it exists on its own terms.

no farewell
to arms

There is a sequence in **Cross of Iron** (Peckinpah, 1976), where Sergeant Steiner (James Coburn) undergoes a period of medical treatment and recuperation at a field hospital after being wounded in battle. While there, he has a fling with a sympathetic nurse, Eva (Senta Berger). In one scene, Eva tries to fathom his military mentality (although Steiner's only loyalty is to his men, it seems that the war is all he has). 'The violence must stop,' Eva declares. Steiner looks at her in disbelief. 'The violence must stop?' he echoes incredulously.

Peckinpah, of course, was (undeservedly) notorious for his portrayal of violence. It is easy to hear in Eva the voice of the 'moral majority', decrying onscreen violence, and in Steiner the world-weary response of the filmmaker – in particular the intelligent filmmaker, for whom the depiction of violence is integral to the film's aesthetic and emotional (and, more often than not, moral) impact.

While it is true that some films feature violence purely for its own sake, there are many reasons for the validity of its use. Primarily, it has the effect of challenging an audience; or a value system; or the establishment.

Complicity: the guilt of the audience

Peeping Tom (Michael Powell, 1960) is one of the most controversial British movies of all time: it opened to not just negative but hateful reviews – 'the only really satisfactory way to dispose of [the film] would be to shovel it up and flush it swiftly down the nearest sewer' (Derek Hill in *The Tribune*); 'the sickest and filthiest film I remember seeing' (Isobel Quigley in *The Spectator*) – and all but finished its director's career. The subject matter was, of course, always going to be problematic: voyeurism, pornography, prostitution and the psychological abuse of a child by his father (worryingly played in the film by Powell and his own son). It was also the first serial killer film, twenty years before cinema-goers were familiar with the term. In fact, it would not be until the Eighties that *Peeping Tom* would be widely shown again (thanks largely to the efforts of cineastes like Martin Scorsese) and its reputation re-evaluated.

Many films contain elements of voyeurism – from *Rear Window* to *Dirty Harry* – but *Peeping Tom* explores the psychology of the condition. Notably, Powell and scriptwriter Leo Marks give it its proper name: scoptophilia – the morbid desire to watch. The scoptophiliac in question, Mark (Carl Boehm), is a socially dysfunctional loner whose trauma at the hands of his father has manifested itself in the crimes he commits in adulthood. He works as cameraman at a film studio, moonlighting in the evenings by shooting 'girlie' pictures in a seedy mock-studio above a newsagent's.

The links between voyeurism and movie-watching are strengthened in the film's key line of dialogue: 'All this filming, it isn't healthy.' Elsewhere, Helen (Anna Massey), the naive young woman who unwisely gets involved with Mark, watches a reel of Super 8 shot by Mark's father. The child is terrorized, his fear caught on celluloid. 'That film – it's horrible,' she says. 'But it's just a film. Isn't it?' The chief pleasure of fiction, no matter the horrors that might occur, is the comfort of knowing that it is just fiction. *Peeping Tom* steadily erodes this illusion of reassurance. Later, when Mark kills a flirtatious stand-in (Moira Shearer), it is on a deserted sound stage, under the shadow of a large movie camera, further blurring the lines between illusion and actuality.

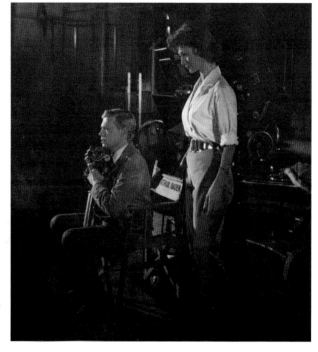

In the shadow of the movie camera: Carl Boehm and Moira Shearer in *Peeping Tom*

More so than the onscreen violence – the killings are effected using a blade extending from one of the feet on Mark's camera tripod – what upset the critics and audiences of the day was the way Powell made them complicit in Mark's deviant acts. From the very first scene, the viewer is forced to watch through Mark's eyes: we walk along a grimy street; a prostitute, her face haggard under too much make up, turns to us. 'It'll be two quid,' she offers. We follow her along a dark passageway, up a flight of steps and into her drab little room. She lights a gas fire. There is nothing remotely erotic in any of this. The leg of the tripod snaps up, our hand reaches out to extend the blade. She screams and backs into a corner. We advance.

The whole sequence is then played out again in black and white, projected onto a screen, as the opening credits appear, somewhat too late to remind us that it's just a film.

99

With the Super 8 of *Peeping Tom* replaced by the camcorder for the video generation, the current trend is for filmmakers to use the 'documentary' format to explore audience fixation/response to scenes of violence. The *bête noire* of American cinema in the year of its release, ***Henry: Portrait of a Serial Killer*** (John McNaughton, 1986), while not strictly presented as a documentary, employs a gritty *cinema verité* style (many scenes have a fly-on-the-wall quality), and in its most controversial scene uses a camcorder to disturbing effect. The scene, presented as grainy point-of-view footage, details the murder of an entire family. The punch line is that it is not in progress as we, the audience, watch it, but being viewed on video by its two perpetrators, Henry (Michael Rooker) and Ottis (Tom Towles). This puts us in the same position as the killers. And it's a grim position to be in.

The murder of the family is often cited as gratuitous in criticism of the film, but it serves a dual purpose. The concept of the family unit is sacrosanct to the average, functional individual. The violation of this concept forces us into a realization of the depth of dysfunctionalism Henry and Ottis personify. Also, there is a dark comparison being drawn. There are three members in the murdered family. So, too, is Henry locked into a domestic situation that involves three people. Only in his case, it is more a warped version of the eternal triangle.

Henry and Ottis are blue collar room-mates, semi-literate, spells in prison behind them. Into their grubby little apartment, all peeling wallpaper and unwashed dishes, comes Becky (Tracy Arnold), Ottis's recently divorced sister. Henry and Becky establish a rapport, largely based on a shared experience of childhood trauma: Becky's sexual abuse at the hands of her father, Henry beaten and forced to wear a dress by his slatternly mother. (A comparison here with *Psycho*. Norman Bates was based on a real-life sociopath, Ed Gein. Likewise, Henry, on Henry Lee Lucas.)

Becky quickly emerges as the only normal member of the household. Again, the effect is twofold. In her conversations with an often reticent Henry, she acts as a surrogate interviewer, asking him about his life and his feelings, trying to understand him (thus heightening the 'documentary' feel). And, in the abuses she has suffered in her past (and will suffer again by the end of the film), she proves that being the product of a dysfunctional background and having violence done to one at a young age do not necessarily mean that one becomes a sociopath in later life.

At the heart of *Henry: Portrait of a Serial Killer* is the notion that the psychopathology of a sociopath cannot be easily pinned down to one conveniently blameworthy event. Becky has suffered the most, but (the breakdown of her marriage notwithstanding) has had the most normal life. Henry, while occasionally polite and sometimes even capable of charm, is embarrassed by intimacy and shies away when Becky offers him her love. Ottis, notwithstanding that his crimes are instigated by Henry, is easily the most reprehensible character in the film. Henry kills people for no better reason than because it's what he does. Ottis does it out of frustration and repression – and enjoys it. His sexual preferences include college boys, his own sister and – in the camcorder sequence – a suggestion of necrophilia.

Henry cannot prevent Ottis from raping Becky by the end of the film. He returns to their apartment to find Ottis trying to strangle her. He intercedes, Ottis overpowering him as they struggle. Becky stabs Ottis in the eye with the sharp end of a steel comb. Henry then uses said instrument to finish the job. He dismembers Ottis in the bath-tub. Wrapped in black bin-liners, the component parts are then dropped from a river bridge. This done, Henry and Becky leave the city together.

True, this doesn't make a romantic hero of a villain the way *Hannibal* does of Lecter (see chapter three), but it does elicit a certain degree of empathy for Henry: with Ottis out of the picture, the city behind him, and the affections of the sympathetic Becky, one feels there might be hope for him.

Not so. Henry and Becky check into a hotel after their first day on the road. Next morning, Henry leaves. Alone.

The word 'portrait' in the title is well chosen. *Henry* is like a documentary but without voiceover; without neat, encapsulating, moralistic soundbites to tell the audience how to think and how to feel. For a film that is capable of producing a strong emotional response, its approach is clinical; distanced. As if a film crew had followed Henry around, discreetly and unobtrusively, and simply observed.

The documentarists in **Man Bites Dog** (Remy Belvaux, Andre Bonzel and Benoit Poelvoorde, 1992), however, are not content simply to observe their subject, Benoit (Poelvoorde). They socialize with him, wining, dining and attending art exhibitions. He entertains them with his versatility on the piano. But as well as being an aesthete, Benoit is racist (he sneers that he once buried 'two Arabs … facing Mecca, of course'), homophobic and a drunkard. He also kills people randomly and without motive. The film crew follow him through (and participate in) a series of murders – he shoots,

Benoit Poelvoorde as a tireless serial killer in *Man Bites Dog*

bludgeons, garrottes and suffocates his victims; he terrifies one elderly lady into a heart attack, musing that he likes to try out new methods and this one apparently saves on bullets. The documentarists' relationship with Benoit vacillates between fractiousness and ingratiation. At one point, they present him with a shoulder holster. Their reward, while he practises his quick-draw skills, is the accidental shooting of one of their number. And he's not the only casualty. Two other crew members are shot in attacks against Benoit. The perpetrator is another serial killer, also being followed by a camera crew.

By the end of the film, Benoit has been arrested, imprisoned and made his escape. Arranging a reunion with his girlfriend, to which he invites the documentary-makers, he is again ambushed. This time he is killed. The film crew are massacred, too, the camera falling to the floor so we can see the cameraman shot down as he tries to run for cover[1].

Henry: Portrait of a Serial Killer and *Man Bites Dog* present violence in a manner designed to prompt the audience into asking themselves why they are watching; what the attraction is. The 'documentary' approach makes it more immediate. Removing a scene of violence from a narrative context, freeing it of cinematic techniques such as editing and slow-motion (which, along with the use of music, can be highly manipulative), can provoke a truer emotional response from the audience. It is then up to the individual to ask themselves how they feel – and, more importantly – how they feel about how they feel.

Which is not to say a conventionally structured film cannot force its audience into an uncomfortable two hours of self-questioning. Almost everything about Michael Haneke's **Funny Games** (1997) assures us that it's only a film: the sumptuous widescreen cinematography, an identifiable genre (hostage/home invasion – familiar from such mainstream fare as *The Desperate Hours*), the progressive escalation of events, the winks and asides the characters make to the camera (at one point they ask the audience if the film has reached a commercial running time yet), and the non-naturalistic manipulation of the medium in a climactic scene where Haneke rewinds the film to replay events differently.

Haneke's dark achievement, whereby he probes his viewers' motivations in their choice of film-going, is twofold. Firstly, he gives his two antagonists absolutely no motive: they take none of the family's top-of-the-range material possessions (the setting is their lakeside summer residence, yacht moored nearby), nor is any ransom demanded; there is no evidence of either of them bearing a grudge; they don't even seem to take any pleasure in their torments. Secondly, every act of violence and/or humiliation (the family pet is killed, the husband's leg broken with his own golf club, the wife forced to disrobe) is not only perpetrated with blank indifference, but also recorded by Haneke's camera in the same vein. That is, when we actually see them. The worst acts of violence – including two of the deaths – occur offscreen.

But even when concentrating on the suggestive rather than the explicit, Haneke gives us nowhere to hide. Things are heard: a thud, screaming, muted voices; all the while, the camera holds on an arbitrary and unnecessarily protracted shot such as the flickering screen of a television or the exterior of the holiday home, not a trace of movement evident in any of its lighted windows. This creates an emotionally ambivalent response in the viewer: a need to know what has happened, and a worry that our worst fears will be confirmed.

Haneke stonily refuses to reward audiences with catharsis. Even when the tables seem to turn on the antagonists, he stops the scene, rewinds the film and re-enacts the events to their advantage with the benefit of hindsight. It's a completely unrealistic moment, but it only increases the atmosphere of dread that permeates the entire film. 'Keep repeating: it's only a movie', the poster for *Last House on the Left* advises. *Funny Games* doesn't even allow us to do this. We know it's just a movie – and this knowledge only makes it worse.

Psychological violence and the transferral of guilt

The films considered so far in this chapter all question the audience: their perception of the acts unfolding onscreen and, by dint of their emotional reaction, their part in them. This approach is one of the most provocative ways a director can use cinema. But, as tabloid hysteria has proven (and continues to prove), there is the risk of the director's intentions being misconstrued, of a film like *Natural Born Killers* being branded as inciting violence when, as we have seen, it actually criticizes the media's obsession with crime, death and human suffering.

Another way of questioning the perception of violence is to confront the main character of the film – conventionally, the 'hero' – with their own response to it; to take them on a journey into their psyche. Jeffrey (Kyle MacLachlan), the protagonist of **Blue Velvet** (David Lynch, 1986), is an innocent. At the outset, a deferential, clean-cut college student, his idyllic worldview is soon destroyed, his innocence corrupted and his own darkness ineffably tapped into. The surface of his picture-postcard hometown (all white picket fences and lush, neatly trimmed gardens) is ripped back to reveal a netherworld of sexual violence and sadomasochism. The catalyst is a severed ear Jeffrey finds in the grass. Initially reporting his macabre discovery to the police, his curiosity drives him to begin his own investigation, aided by Sandy (Laura Dern), the daughter of a local police officer. The trail leads to sultry nightclub singer Dorothy Vallens (Isabella Rossellini). Jeffrey gains access to her apartment, ostensibly to look for clues. It is when she returns from her spot at the club earlier than anticipated that Jeffrey, graduating from illegal

Dennis Hopper as the psychopathic Frank Booth in *Blue Velvet*

entry to voyeurism, bears witness to her twisted sexual relationship with the psychotic Frank Booth (Dennis Hopper). Frank is a portrait in grotesquery: he snorts ether from a face mask, spews profanity, approaches violence and sex with the same remorseless intensity and obsesses over the lyrics to Roy Orbison's 'In Dreams'.

Frank, it transpires, is a hardened criminal in cohorts with a crooked cop. He is holding Dorothy's husband (it is to him the ear belongs) and son hostage, forcing her to pander to his warped fantasies. By the time Jeffrey realizes the depth of Dorothy's involvement with Frank – not to mention the violence of which Frank is capable – he has become sexually involved with Dorothy himself. Events take a nasty turn with the implication of Dorothy's complicity: during sex, she insists he hit her. Shocked, he at first refuses. But he soon complies, striking her twice. By now, Jeffrey has discovered a core of darkness inside himself – his inner Frank, as it were.

Things take a nastier turn yet: Frank discovers his liaisons with Dorothy and takes Jeffrey on a 'joyride', which ends at a gravel pit. Jeffrey has been mocked and bullied by Frank's comrades all night; now he is sexually humiliated by Frank himself and savagely beaten. 'You are fucking lucky to be alive,' Frank tells him. When Jeffrey stumbles out of the gravel pit the following morning, face swollen with bruises, mouth and nose caked with dried blood – and later when he sits alone in his room, weeping for the things he's seen and his own complicity – one feels that his life probably isn't worth that much anymore.

Jeffrey's guilt and sense of degradation are painful enough. Worse is the understanding of the self that Mark Daly (David Hemmings) comes to by the end of **Deep Red** (Dario Argento, 1975). Like Jeffrey, his personality, if not necessarily heroic (he spends much of the film in a state of nervous agitation that borders on cowardice), certainly seems sympathetic: he is a musician, has a social conscience (witnessing a murder at the start of the film, he puts aside his fears for his own safety and rushes to the scene to help the victim) and frets about his friend Carlo (Gabriele Lavia), a repressed homosexual who is sliding into alcoholism. Also like Jeffrey, he begins his own investigation. His motives are just as questionable, and the effects even more devastating.

Warned by several concerned friends to return to his native England until the case is solved, he persists in trying to unmask the killer himself, even though he is menaced by an unseen prowler while he rehearses alone in his studio apartment. Teaming up with investigative journalist Gianna (Daria Nicolodi), he pieces together a series of clues surrounding the murder victim, Helga Ulman (Macha Meril), a medium who was about to reveal the truth about an unsolved murder dating back a couple of decades. He uncovers two significant leads: a parapsychologist who worked with Helga, and an author on famous homicide cases. Both are murdered before they can impart any information to Mark. These extended set-pieces are operatic in concept and explicit in their detail. The author is terrorized in her home, bludgeoned and drowned in a tub of boiling water, her face deformed by blisters by the time she expires. The parapsychologist is overpowered, his face driven repeatedly into the sharp corner of a marble table top, teeth smashed and mouth bloodied, before a blade is driven through his neck.

Finally, all other leads terminated, Mark and Gianna uncover a tangible piece of evidence in an old school; evidence that points to Mark's friend Carlo. They are attacked, Gianna sustaining serious wounding. Carlo hesitates when he has Mark at gunpoint, then flees the scene as police arrive. He bungles his escape, catching his leg in a chain trailing behind a refuse truck: he is dragged along the street for several hundred yards before being swung out in front of an oncoming car.

Reeling from his death, it takes Mark some time to realize that he had parted company with Carlo only moments before he witnessed the original murder. Baffled, he returns to the scene. Here, he is attacked by Carlo's psychologically unstable mother, Marta (Clara Calamai), a former actress forced to abandon her profession by her domineering husband. It transpires she murdered him out of resentment, a crime the prepubescent Carlo witnessed and has been disturbed by ever since. Marta is responsible for two deaths: her husband and, twenty years later, Helga. The others were committed by Carlo, simultaneously wanting to protect Marta's secret and to prevent Mark from finding out (and therefore having to kill him). Driven, in other words, by two misguided forms of love: familial for his mother and platonic for his friend.

Mark is only spared from death when Marta's ornamental necklace is caught in the mechanism of a descending elevator, and she is decapitated. The final image is one of terrible realization: staring at his reflection in the dark mirror of Marta's blood, Mark is faced with the knowledge that two people have died because of his persistent, clumsy efforts at detection.

FX and violence: the horror film

The protracted, bloody deaths in *Deep Red* are typical of the horror genre's emphasis on explicit imagery. Although there have been notable films which have abandoned the visceral in favour of the implicit – from Robert Wise's *The Haunting* (1963) to Alejandro Amenabar's *The Others* (2001) – the general trend is towards gore. For this reason, special effects have always been at the forefront of horror movies.

Two films in particular exemplify the visceral impact of special effects. David Cronenberg's **Scanners** (1980) broke new ground with its legendary exploding head scene. The horror in most of

Cronenberg's films emanates from the human body: sexuality, disease and mutation are variously explored in *Shivers* (1974), *Rabid* (1976) and *Videodrome* (1982), while *The Brood* (1979) reimagines the miracle of birth in the terms of nightmare. *Scanners* centres around a group of telekinetics who are capable of invading the minds and controlling the thoughts of others. Two factions, one acting for a shadowy government agency, the other a band of freedom fighters, come into conflict. The use of the mind as a weapon is established from the off. A conference pertaining to telekinesis, with a demonstration courtesy of a 'scanner', turns into a duel, resolved when the weaker combatant's head bursts messily across the audience.

The infamous exploding head scene in David Cronenberg's *Scanners*

It remains a startling moment, over 20 years on. Less an example of special effects for their own sake, it establishes the notion of mind-rape, a concept revisited when a driver is compelled to run his own car off the road and a guard made to turn his gun on himself. The film unfolds within a framework that is a hybrid of the horror, sci-fi and thriller genres, but Cronenberg uses this framework to debate matters of free will, personal freedom and state-sanctioned intrusion upon the individual. The finale has antagonists from both sides squaring off against each other, the drama heightened by the revelation that they are brothers. In their final duel, Cronenberg provides a pointer towards another genre: *Scanners* is essentially a western, only with telepathic shoot-outs instead of the six-gun variety.

John Carpenter's **The Thing** (1982) also has a touch of the western about it, this time the homestead-under-siege sub-genre[2]. Here, the setting is a polar ice station crewed by Americans, whose cushy (if cold) lifestyles are intruded upon by a husky dog, which, unbeknown to them, is host to an alien life-form. A Norwegian research team, their number decimated by the being, has already tried to kill the host, but have succeeded only in exploding their helicopter and killing themselves. The dog is taken into the American ice station and all hell, as the saying has it, breaks loose.

The twist on the siege situation is that the scientists find themselves under threat from within. The creature, after a hideous manifestation as it bursts out of the body of its host, is quickly able to assimilate the qualities and appearance of its next victim. The most gruesome scene in the film has one of the men suffer heart failure. Emergency measures are taken. A defibrillation unit is utilized. As the charge is applied, his chest opens into a gaping cavity into which the hands of the medical officer sink. A set of serrations where his ribs should be close over them and the unfortunate medico, jerking back in horror, is left with two stumps gushing blood. As with *Scanners*, the effect (pre Computer Generated Imagery) has lost none of its power to startle.

The Thing is one of the few horror films that goes all out in the effects department without sacrificing tension or character development. In fact, it is with the character interrelationships that the film comes into its own, developing into an effective study of mistrust and paranoia, and has the courage of its convictions to see its theme through to a fittingly downbeat conclusion.

Horror rooted in society is at the heart of George A Romero's 'Dead' trilogy. **Night of the Living Dead** (1969) depicts nothing less than a complete breakdown of all social conventions. It begins with a brother and sister visiting their parents' graves. The solemnity of the occasion and the hallowed ground of the churchyard are intruded upon by a lumbering zombie. The film's nominal protagonist is killed immediately, leaving his sister, Barbara (Judith O'Dea) to flee for her life.

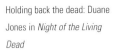

Holding back the dead: Duane Jones in *Night of the Living Dead*

108

Romero has signalled his intent from the opening frames and he continues to subvert genre conventions and audience expectations. Barbara takes refuge in an isolated farmhouse, where she is joined by a disparate group of individuals; soon they are besieged by zombies. Ben (Duane Jones), a black man (stereotypically the sacrificial supporting character in many genre films), proves the strongest character. A young couple (usually the main characters in genre films pitched at the teenage market) who stage a daring escape attempt are summarily killed off as their plan ends in disaster.

As they struggle to hold off the zombies (Romero offers only the briefest of explanations – some sort of virus from outer space – as to the sudden proliferation of flesh-eating reanimated corpses), gangs of shotgun-toting rednecks roam the countryside, treating the crisis as one big turkey-shoot. (It is quickly established that burning or a shot to the head is the only sure-fire means of dispatching a zombie.)

In essence, *Night of the Living Dead* divides society into two factions: zombies (shambolic, slow-moving, but ultimately able to overpower through sheer weight of numbers) and vigilantes (shambolic, beer-guzzling gun owners). Caught between the two are the beleaguered souls in the farmhouse. Barbara and Ben alone survive the zombies' siege. They emerge from the farmhouse, in a grim coda, only to be mistaken for the living dead by a trigger-happy redneck and gunned down.

Dawn of the Dead (1979) substitutes its predecessor's rural locale for a huge shopping mall on the outskirts of a large city. Four survivors seek sanctuary there, touching down on the roof in a stolen helicopter. They secure the entrances and exits, locking and barricading them securely, and utilize a couple of delivery trucks abandoned in the parking area to seal off the delivery bays. Raiding a gun shop, they take care of the zombies still inside the mall. Their gleeful hunt and kill expeditions, during which they run rings around their shuffling antagonists, set the tone for the middle section of the film, where (having defeated not only the zombies but a marauding gang of bikers[3]) they have the run of the mall, all they want of consumer goods and foodstuff theirs for the taking. Zombie movie it may be, but *Dawn of the Dead* develops into one of the most effective satires on materialism ever committed to film. The survivors lapse into a life of self-contained luxury (one of them enthuses over a top-of-the-range rifle liberated from the gun shop, remarking, 'The only person who could miss with this is the asshole who could afford it'), while the living dead batter away at the doors outside.

There are only four survivors – three men, one woman. Naturally, internal tensions surface. Emotions run high. The human condition is effectively juxtaposed with the impassive onslaught of the living dead, who finally force their way into the mall and over-run it. By the end of the film, only two of the survivors remain, unable to hold off the zombies any longer. They retreat to the roof-top and the helicopter, reluctantly taking off even though they know that fuel is low and their destination uncertain.

The small band of survivors in
Dawn of the Dead

Night of the Living Dead and *Dawn of the Dead* share the same sense of self-containment, their protagonists facing up as much to their own demons as to the horde of zombies gathering outside. The milieu of **Day of the Dead** (1985) is even more claustrophobic. Set virtually in its entirety in an underground military bunker, much of the film documents a stand-off between a team of scientists trying to study the zombies and the military personnel who simply want to engage them in battle as they would an invading army. The military are essentially the rednecks of the first instalment but with training and better equipment. Not that either of these stand them in any stead when the zombies finally gain ingress. The last half hour of the film comprises Romero's goriest cinematic work, an almost constant spate of dismemberment and disembowelment.

Prior to this, the science/militarism debate is played out against the scientists' attempts to humanize a captured zombie. At one point, the creature, recognizing a soldier's rank, salutes him. In the climactic massacre, this selfsame zombie demonstrates its ability to use a pistol.

One of the characters in *Dawn of the Dead* speculates on whether the zombies are drawn back to the mall because they have some deep-rooted memory of visiting such places while they were alive. When the zombie arms himself in *Day of the Dead*, this notion is revisited. How much longer, Romero seems to be asking, before they remember how to use other weapons, how to use transport, how to organize themselves? Throughout the course of the trilogy, small bastions of humanity have holed up in rural/agricultural, materialist/consumerist and military/scientific environments and have been defeated, from within and without, in each case.

Social protest

If one defines 'the establishment' as any class- or authority-based system, the values of which are offered as a social blueprint or imposed upon society wholesale, then Lindsay Anderson's *If...* (1968) pretty much takes on the establishment in its entirety. The setting is a public school (i.e. a private one) where the emphasis on routine, inspections and discipline is akin to that of a military institution. This parallel is augmented in a scene where the pupils don khaki uniforms and participate in a 'war games' exercise. The church is represented by the interminable services attended by staff and pupils alike. The staff symbolize the upper echelons of society, paying lip service to the church; the prefects are the parvenus and nouveau riche, indulging in vulgar little power plays while paying lip service to those above them; the rest of the pupils represent the lower classes, told what to do, when to do it and most resolutely where their place is.

The individual – the rebel, the free-thinker – is represented by Travis (Malcolm McDowell) and a small cluster of like-minded friends. Their non-conformism is apparent in the pictures of guerrillas (including the iconic image of Che Guevara) with which their walls are decorated.

Rooftop rebellion: Travis (Malcolm McDowell) opens fire in *If...*

The bulk of the film depicts the abuses of the establishment against the individual. In one scene, Travis is made to stand naked under a cold shower. Later, he and his friends are ordered to report to the gym, where they are flogged for insubordinate behaviour. Travis receives more blows than the others, and is then obliged to thank his antagonist for it. The metaphor is clear: the individual having to take what the establishment doles out – the beating is as much a stand-in for the legal or penal system (laws, regulations, punishment, imprisonment) as it is for the abuses against the civil liberties of the activist or protestor – and be thankful for it.

The film's message of social protest is spelled out in its denouement in the strongest terms possible – terms of revolution and guerrilla warfare. Travis and his comrades sabotage a service at which a General (a stuffy 'Colonel Blimp'-type whose alma mater is the school) is giving a speech. A planted canister fills the hall with noxious fumes. As the congregation – their number including members of the education system, the clergy and the forces, as well as a royal visitor – stumble outside, they are fired upon. From the vantage point of an adjacent rooftop, Travis and co. use machine-guns, mortars and grenades to mow down swathes of them.

A counter-attack is mounted; gunfire returned. In a moment that says much about the repressed violence of 'polite' society, an old lady in a floral-print frock and an Ascot-style hat angles a Bren gun towards them, shouting 'Bastards! Bastards!', as she fires off a round.

As the film ends, the counter-attack redoubles, suggesting that the rebels will soon be overcome by superior numbers. But, undaunted, they keep on firing … . The screen turns black.

The *Evening News* described *If...* as 'a hand grenade of a film', and it certainly is incendiary. Anderson's subsequent attacks on society, *O Lucky Man!* (1973) and *Britannia Hospital* (1982), utilized, respectively, Brechtian fantasy and over-the-top satire, but to somewhat lesser effect. *If...* remains Anderson's best work. It sent shockwaves through British cinema and British society, and more than 30 years on has lost none of its power.

Chinatown: Jake Gittes (Jack Nicholson) pays the price for poking his nose in

If... is a uniquely British film in its incisive dissection of the class system, the old-school-tie network. Social protest in American cinema, where structures of hierarchy are based more on money and political connections, is generally aimed at the government and big business. **Chinatown** (Roman Polanski, 1974) is set in Los Angeles in the Thirties and evokes the spirit of film noir in its period trappings, its complex plot and its hard-bitten anti-hero Jake Gittes (Jack

Nicholson), a man not above slapping a woman around to get information.

Gittes is a private eye, the mainstay of whose business is taking compromising photographs in divorce cases. Hired by a jealous woman to uncover the sexual improprieties of her husband, Hollis Mulwray (Darrell Zwerling), a prominent engineer overseeing the provision of water to the city, he dutifully digs the dirt, only to find his seedy snaps smeared across the front pages. The realization that he has been used hits home when he is visited by the real Mrs Mulwray (Faye Dunaway), who threatens him with a lawsuit. Thus he sets out to find who has set him up, and is drawn into a labyrinthine conspiracy involving water rights, crooked politicians and an incest scandal. It is arch-villain Noah Cross (John Huston), who encapsulates the film's detestation of politicos, when, alluding to himself, he says, 'Politicians, ugly buildings and whores all get respectable if they last long enough.'

And Cross is determined to last. He throws stumbling-blocks and fires warning shots across Gittes's path throughout. In a particularly gruesome scene, Gittes is warned off by a gang of thugs, one of whom is barely knee-high to a grasshopper. 'Where'd you get the dwarf?' Gittes wisecracks, but he's not laughing when, moments later, the vertically challenged individual (played by Polanski himself), produces a knife and slits Gittes's nose. (Not only an excruciating moment of torture, but a metaphor for the inherent 'nosiness' of Gittes's profession.)

The ending is unbearably downbeat: having uncovered Cross's crimes – the murderous acquisition of the Los Angeles water rights; the fathering of an illegitimate child by his own daughter – Gittes is unable to do a thing. Forcibly detained by his nemesis on the police force, Lieutenant Escobar (who, it is intimated, is in Cross's pocket), Cross is able to have Evelyn Mulwray (for it is she who is his daughter) taken away before the scandal can be made public. As Cross exits the picture, his seat of power secure, Escobar begrudgingly turns Gittes loose. 'Forget it, Jake, it's Chinatown,' runs the devastating pay-off line, Chinatown becoming a metaphor for the kind of place where laws and conventional morality do not apply – i.e. the province of the rich, powerful and well-connected.

The government is the villain-by-default of *Bonnie and Clyde*, even though not a single politician puts in an appearance. Although its eponymous protagonists are outlaws, the backdrop of the Great Depression elevates them to folk heroes: they're young, glamorous, defy the law and, at one point, divide the takings from their latest heist among the impoverished citizens queuing at the bank. And this during a period of national economic depletion and political distrust, when a popular joke of the time was 'don't tell my mother I'm in politics, she thinks I play piano in a whorehouse'. When the charismatic lovers and partners-in-crime meet their bullet-sprayed, slow-motion demise, the effect is not so much the catharsis of, say, Peckinpah's *The Wild Bunch*, as a poeticized moment of martyrdom.

As discussed in chapter three, *Bonnie and Clyde* heralded an era of filmmaking which was anti-establishment. *Chinatown* was made only a few years later. Although period films, both were contemporary in their attitude. Other films of the time, contemporarily set, were even more up-front: *The Parallax View* (Alan J Pakula, 1974), *Three Days of the Condor* (Sidney Pollack, 1975) and *All the President's Men* (Pakula, 1976) are all nakedly critical of the political system.

Counter-culture also provides a frame of reference for American films of social protest. **Easy Rider** (Dennis Hopper, 1969) is just as anti-establishment as any of its more politically motivated contemporaries. Its hippie protagonists, Billy (Hopper) and Captain America (Peter Fonda)[4], begin the film by making a profitable drug deal, then use the proceeds to fund an aimless odyssey across the States. For all their amorality and functionless lives, their road trip (in both senses of the word) is an exercise in iconography, as they cut across huge vistas of emptiness on their gleaming, low-slung Harley Davidsons, Steppenwolf's 'Born to be Wild' rumbling away on the soundtrack. En route to nowhere, they score dope and sexual favours in a cemetery, meet up with George Hanson (Jack Nicholson), an alcoholic lawyer (indicative of someone within the system who has become disenchanted by it), and opine 'this used to be a great country'.

Easy Rider is a film of its time, its hallucinatory vision of a stoner's lifestyle perfectly realized in the infamous graveyard sequence. Its real stroke of brilliance, though, is its ending. Apropos of nothing, two rednecks in a pick-up truck turn their shotguns on Billy and Captain America, destroying their bikes and killing them. This sudden and unexpected turn (up till this point, the film has played as a warped celebration of their iconoclastic lifestyle) emphasizes the prejudices the hippie movement was faced with. Billy and Captain America dare to live life according to their own standards, to use drugs recreationally, to buck the system and criticize their country and not be involved in the Vietnam conflict.

114

Interestingly, the system (which, inevitably, makes them pay) is here represented by the two shotgun-wielding rednecks. Their weapons are indicative of pro-militarism; their detestation of the hippies is indicative of society's mistrust of youth – particularly youth which thinks for itself and, having thought, decides its best option is simply to get stoned. (The hippies are middle-aged and determinedly non-thinkers.)

The flipside to Billy and Captain America's freewheeling, narcotic-fuelled life (and death) is demonstrated, in no less graphic terms, in ***Midnight Express*** (Alan Parker, 1978), in which the penal system comes under scrutiny. The film is based on actual events, the facts of which – a young American is incarcerated in a Turkish jail – allow the filmmakers the opportunity of depicting prison as (quite literally) a different world. The culture/language barrier also makes for immediate empathy, as the narrative takes on the quality of an 'innocent abroad' morality tale. Not that Billy Hayes (Brad Davis) is all that innocent. He is apprehended at the airport with a couple of dozen blocks of hashish wrapped in silver foil and taped to his body. But does the punishment fit the crime? Even the most strident anti-drugs campaigner would surely find Billy's ordeal a little undue. Mistreatment begins while he is awaiting trial: he is blindfolded, beaten with clubs, bound and hoisted up feet first and beaten on the souls of his feet.

The trial is over quickly. He is found guilty of possession and sent down for four years and two months. The prosecution is less than

An innocent abroad? Billy Hayes (Brad Davis) takes a beating in *Midnight Express*

115

happy with this and, while Billy serves his sentence, the case is referred to a new court. This time he is found guilty of smuggling and a harsher sentence is passed: 30 years.

By now Billy has befriended fellow American Jimmy (Randy Quaid) and Englishman Max (John Hurt). Both have suffered abuses: Max's cat has been hanged, and an escape attempt by Jimmy has been rewarded with a beating resulting in a hernia and the loss of a testicle. Nonetheless, another escape is planned. When their efforts are uncovered, Jimmy is hauled off for another beating (he has been betrayed by a Turkish inmate) which ruptures his hernia. Billy beats the turncoat to death in retribution, as a consequence of which is he worked over by the guards, then transferred to an area of the prison designated for the criminally insane. Not that any treatment for their condition is offered; they are simply encouraged to walk in interminable circles, sinking deeper into their madness.

Billy clings on to his sanity, though. Using money smuggled into the jail by his parents, he bribes the warder (the man responsible for Max's injuries) to transfer him to the infirmary, a minimally guarded wing, reputed to be easy to break out of. However, the warder hauls him off instead to the guardroom, intent on homosexually raping him. Billy kills the warder in self-defence and finally effects the longed-for escape disguised in his uniform.

Andrei Konchalovsky's **_Runaway Train_** (1985) starts with a prison break, from a maximum security penitentiary in Alaska. Manny (Jon Voight) is released from solitary confinement after three years when a court rules that his having been welded in constitutes a violation of his rights. So begins a battle of wills with prison warder Frank Barstow (Kyle T Heffner), a man very much in the vein of _Unforgiven_'s Little Bill, who believes that all criminals are scum and deserve nothing but the most vicious treatment.

Manny's outlook on life is no less stoical than Frank's. Early on, Manny quotes Nietzsche – 'what doesn't kill me makes me stronger' – and the film soon establishes itself as a pared down, hard-as-nails existentialist thriller whose antagonists are different sides of the same coin, Manny as the individual ('I'm at war with the world and everyone in it'), Frank representing the system. Both are intractable. No quarter is asked or given by either.

Almost immediately Manny leaves solitary, there is an attempt on his life, a prisoner in the pay of Frank going at him with a shiv. Manny is stabbed through the hand, but fights back. His attacker is knifed in the back and killed by a lifer sympathetic to Manny. As the guards step in, rifles brandished, Manny taunts them, daring them to shoot him.

The incident spurs him to an escape attempt – a successful one, notwithstanding the unwanted presence of brash loudmouth Buck (Eric Roberts). The pair then face an inhospitable landscape and sub-zero weather conditions. Arriving at a marshalling yard, they opportunistically climb aboard a train (made up of four hulking great diesel locomotives) and settle back. This is where their luck runs out. The engineer, keeling over from a heart attack, plunges out of the cab, and the train – brakes burned away, the power cut-off inoperable from all but the lead locomotive – hurtles across the tundra at an ever-increasing speed.

As the railroad authorities try to divert the train, Manny and Buck find they are not alone in their plight. Railroad worker Sara (Rebecca de Mornay), dodging work by napping in one of the locomotives, is also on board. An ordinary person in extraordinary circumstances, it is against her that Manny and Buck are contrasted. Buck, despite his adolescent behaviour, comes off the better, at least demonstrating some form of emotional empathy towards her. Manny's outlook, on the other hand, just becomes more nihilistic:

> **Sara:** You're an animal.
> **Manny:** No, worse – human.

The finale has Frank lowered by helicopter onto the speeding train even as it is diverted onto a dead-end line where its crash and the deaths of all on board will be inevitable. Manny and Frank go head-to-head. Manny disarms Frank of his gun, discharging a fire extinguisher into his face and then using the cylinder to bludgeon him. Securing him to a generator with his own handcuffs, Manny refuses to trigger the power cut-off. He uncouples the lead engine from the other three, saving Buck and Sara's lives, then takes to the roof of the locomotive, arms held aloft in bitter triumph, as he and Frank thunder towards their death, the snowstorm engulfing them.

A different form of institutional violence, perhaps even more distressing in that the inmates are not criminals but ordinary people who have become afflicted by mental illness, surfaces in **One Flew Over the Cuckoo's Nest** (Milos Forman, 1975). The one exception, who is neither insane nor blameless in his incarceration, is

The individual against the system: McMurphy (Jack Nicholson) faces up to Nurse Ratched (Louise Fletcher) in *One Flew over the Cuckoo's Nest*

Randall P McMurphy (Jack Nicholson). Serving time for statutory rape, he feigns insanity in order to effect a transfer to the asylum; his period of evaluation there equates to time off work detail at the prison. Essentially, he bucks one system only to come up against another, here personified by Nurse Ratched (Louise Fletcher). A petty bureaucratic tyrant, she keeps her patients firmly subjugated, exploiting their insecurities.

McMurphy's determination to undermine her authority ensures his popularity with the 'inmates', particularly the stoic and uncommunicative Chief Bromden (Will Sampson), an enigmatic Indian whose size and strength belie his inability to cope with the world, and the congenitally shy teenager Billy Bobbit (Brad Dourif). McMurphy's escapades progress from organizing card games and arguing with Nurse Ratched over access to a television for coverage of the World Series, to hijacking the hospital bus and taking his companions out for a day of deep-sea fishing.

When his behaviour results in a riot in the day room and a fight with the porters, he is subjected to electric-shock treatment. As with Noah Cross in *Chinatown*, Nurse Ratched has the full weight of the system behind her, and the system will forever be more powerful than the individual.

And yet it is outrage over the violated rights of the individual – Billy – that causes McMurphy to seal his own fate. Planning an escape from the asylum, he throws himself a farewell party, bribing a trustee to smuggle in a couple of girls and few bottles of spirits. Billy, desperately self-conscious and afflicted by chronic stuttering, thanks McMurphy for his friendship. McMurphy, deciding that the lad would benefit more from getting laid than from any form of therapy, sets him up with his white trash girlfriend. Billy proves receptive to her charms. While McMurphy, booze-addled, waits for him to get finished, he drifts off to sleep. Nurse Ratched's arrival the following morning is the very definition of a rude awakening. The situation deteriorates when she discovers Billy *in flagrante delecto*:

Nurse Ratched: Aren't you ashamed?

Billy: No, I'm not.

Nurse Ratched: You know, Billy, what worries me is how your mother is going to take this.

She orders the porters to haul him off to the doctor's office, and the ensuing commotion provides McMurphy with a chance for escape. Before he can take it, he is alerted by screams. Billy has used a piece of broken glass to commit suicide. McMurphy flips and attacks Nurse Ratched, wrestling her to the floor as he tries to strangle her. A porter intervenes; a cosh to the back of the head lays McMurphy out.

The individual has taken his last stand against the system, and now the system destroys him: further applications of electric-shock treatment render him a vegetable. In an act of mercy killing, Chief Bromden puts him out of his misery, smothering him with a pillow, then breaks out of the asylum, disappearing into the night. As with the deaths of Bonnie and Clyde, McMurphy's demise has about it the inspirational quality of a martyrdom.

In Spike Lee's **Do the Right Thing** (1989), the death of Radio Raheem (Bill Nunn) at the hands of white police officers accords martyrdom to a character previously treated as a social pariah by the very members of the community who use his death to instigate a riot. The action takes place during a sweltering day in Brooklyn, the heat only serving to exacerbate an already palpable air of hostility. The black, Hispanic, Korean and Italian elements all bear grudges against each other. The white cops are equally bigoted.

Differences of opinion degenerate into violence when Radio – so-called for the oversized ghetto-blaster he carries around, Public Enemy incessantly thumping out of the speakers – joins forces with the militant Buggin Out (Giancarlo Esposito) against Sal (Danny Aiello), the Italian-American owner of the local pizzeria who is racially prejudiced even though all of his clientele are black. Delivery boy Mookie (Lee) adopts the thankless mantle of mediator between Buggin Out, Sal, and Sal's even more blatantly racist son Pino (John Turturro). But even he is finally alienated by Sal's attitude. When blows are exchanged between Radio and Sal, the inevitable crowd gathering as violence erupts, Mookie is first to hurl a dustbin through the window of the pizzeria.

The police intercede. Their use of force in restraining Radio goes beyond the acceptable: he dies at their hands. They bundle his corpse into the back of a squad car and depart the scene. The mob, most of whom have previously denigrated Radio for his anti-social behaviour, decry his murder and vent their frustrations on Sal's pizzeria, razing it to the ground.

Throughout the film, Lee realistically refuses to simplify his depiction of racial conflict. Everyone has his or her own grievance. Equally, everyone is capable of prejudice or misunderstanding. *Do the Right Thing* is less a polemic about race than a study of human nature and human frailty. Lee creates a sense of ambivalence that carries over into the closing credits, where he quotes Martin Luther King – 'violence as a way of achieving racial justice is both impractical and immoral ... violence is immoral because it thrives on hatred rather than love ... violence ends by defeating itself' – and Malcolm X – 'you and I have to preserve the right to do what is necessary ... it doesn't mean that I advocate violence, but at the same time I am not against using violence in self-defence. I don't even call it violence when it's self-defence. I call it intelligence'.

These quotations seem to contradict each other. But they both make sense.

Where *Do the Right Thing* examines racial violence from a multiplicity of ethnic viewpoints, Tony Kaye's ***American History X*** (1999) probes the mindset of the white supremacy movement. Set in Venice Beach, it chronicles the homecoming of Derek Vinyard (Edward Norton), newly released from prison on a manslaughter charge, and the effects his return has on his brother Danny (Edward Furlong), a high school kid in danger of going down the same road that led to Derek's incarceration.

Derek's racial prejudices are nurtured by his father, a firemen, who is subsequently shot by a black youth when attending an emergency call in a ghetto area. His rage and loss lead him to involvement with a neo-Nazi group, through whose ranks he swiftly rises. Events come to a head when Danny alerts him to a group of black youths trying to steal his car. Derek shoots two of them, killing one and wounding the other, while the third escapes. Derek drags the wounded youth, sprawled in the road, over to the pavement and tells him to put his mouth on the kerb. Terrified, a gun to his head, the youth complies, his teeth jutting out on the kerbstone. Derek straightens up, then stamps on the back of his head. As the police arrive to arrest him, Derek displays no emotion, kneeling in the middle of the road, shirtless and smirking, his chest decorated with a large tattoo of a swastika.

During his imprisonment, Danny becomes drawn into the same milieu, the white supremacists welcoming him with open arms, his brother a hero in their eyes. When Derek is released, however, he is a changed man. Two crucial events have happened to him inside. Disenchantment with the penitentiary's neo-Nazi contingent (he realizes that the ringleader, while spouting racist propaganda, is scoring drugs from ethnic prisoners to peddle to his white followers) is compounded when a group of white cons attack and homosexually rape him in the showers. While he is recovering in the prison infirmary, Dr Sweeney (Avery Brooks), the African-American principle of Derek's former school (and now Danny's teacher) visits him to voice his concerns over Danny's increasingly right-wing beliefs. Brutalized, weakened, vulnerable, Derek is faced with a truth he cannot escape when Sweeney confronts him about the choices he has made. 'Has anything you've done,' Sweeney challenges him, 'made your life better?' Derek tries to hold back tears as he silently shakes his head.

With Derek up for parole, Sweeney puts in a word for him on condition that he convinces Danny of the error of his ways. Danny initially resists, drawn towards the fellowship of the white supremacists and his popularity among them. Eventually, though, proffering his humiliations in prison as a cautionary tale, Derek persuades him of the dangers to the self that the hatred of others provokes. Tragically, he is proved right – his own redemption having come too late to save his brother's life – when Danny is shot at school by a black youth he had earlier challenged in a race-related stand-off. 'What have I done?' Derek weeps as he clutches Danny's body, weighed down with the realization that this act of violence was the product of his prejudice.

War and anti-militarism

The war film falls into three distinct categories: propaganda; big-budget, jingoistic Boy's Own action spectaculars; and films that consider the morality of war – the inhumanity it entails, the waste of life. Studio output of the former, of course, is generally confined to actual periods of conflict. The most notable efforts came out of World War II.

Michael Powell's **49th Parallel** (1941) was financed by the Ministry of Information as an exercise in appealing for American involvement in the war. The narrative centres on the survivors of an German U-boat sunk off the coast of Canada and their efforts to reach the eponymous geographical point, take advantage of America's neutrality and petition for repatriation. Their journey is marked by acts of violence – they randomly open fire on the Eskimo community at the trading post to which they come ashore; they abuse the shelter offered them by a sojourning English anthropologist (Leslie Howard), tying him up and destroying his collection of books and paintings – but none is as shocking as the murder of one of their own. The incident occurs at a Hutterite camp where the good-natured Vogel (Niall MacGinnis) rediscovers his old profession as a baker and expresses a desire to stay behind and join the commune. He is taken out at dawn and shot, the retort sounding off screen as the fanatical Lieutenant Hirth (Eric Portman) makes the Nazi salute.

This typifies the violence inflicted by the Nazis: brutal, cold and cowardly, usually by the gun. The violence inflicted upon them is just, provoked and cathartic; in two key scenes (one detailing the anthropologist's revenge, the other involving an AWOL American soldier), it is doled out by fist, the Nazis proving themselves weak and unmanly once disarmed.

If *49th Parallel* is a call to arms, **Went the Day Well?** (Alberto Cavalcanti, 1942) is both a warning against Fifth Columnists and a celebration of 'home front' activities. It begins with the arrival in a sleepy village of a German platoon disguised in British uniforms. They are the vanguard of a planned Nazi invasion; it is their task to secure the village for use as a communication headquarters. They move quickly. Home guard organizer Oliver Wilsford (Leslie Banks), a Nazi sympathizer, clandestinely assists them, all the while playing the affronted patriot for the benefit of his fellow residents (although he later knifes an erstwhile friend in the back to prevent his cover from being blown).

The villagers are rounded up and imprisoned in the church, a would-be safe haven recast, with grim irony, as a makeshift internment camp; the sense of sacrilege is compounded when the priest is shot in the back. The switchboard operator is instructed to inform all callers the lines are down – an order backed up by a savage blow to the face. The village is sealed off by barricades. Cyclists and walkers are redirected. A Home Guard patrol is fired on; one of them keels over, blood gushing from his eye.

The Germans are unsparing in their use of force (they plan the execution of children as reprisal for an escape attempt). But so too, when the chance for resistance arises, are the villagers. The old dear from the post office, every inch the whimsical maiden aunt, throws pepper in her guard's eyes and, as he gropes about blindly, strikes him with an axe. It is a moment of almost horror movie iconography, her entire form filling the frame as she brings the instrument down, and is made less palatable when, seconds later, a second German effects retribution by running her through with a bayonet. More cathartic is the moment when vicar's daughter Nora (Valerie Taylor), discovering Wilsford's treachery, coldly empties the contents of a handgun into him.

Went the Day Well? offers as much in the way of grim determination as it does propagandist messaging. This is evident from the outset. A framing device has a villager describe the events in retrospect. The opening line is 'after the war was over and Hitler and his lot got what was coming to them ... .' This from a film made in 1942, before the tide of the war had turned in the Allies' favour!

The framing scenes which bookend Steven Spielberg's **Schindler's List** (1993) remind the audience that although fifty years have passed since the events depicted, it is still within the lifetime of the survivors. The film opens with a simple ceremony in a Jewish household and ends with the placing of stones on Oskar Schindler's grave by the Jews, still alive at the film's release, who survived the concentration camp at Plaszow because of Schindler's efforts.

The face of tyranny: Ralph Fiennes as Amon Goeth in *Schindler's List*

Adapted from Thomas Kenneally's fact-based novel *Schindler's Ark*, its protagonist is by no means a moral crusader. Schindler (Liam Neeson) is a fully paid-up member of the Nazi party and a ruthless businessman – every inch a war-profiteer. His privileged lifestyle – glamorous wife, glitzy parties, behind-the-scenes deals with Nazi top brass – is in stark contrast to the disenfranchisement of the Jews. Schindler witnesses their sufferings first hand: the ghetto in which they are rehoused is visible from his enamel factory in Krakow. The ghetto is later sacked by Nazi stormtroopers and the Jews packed off to death camps. Again, Schindler is witness to the atrocity.

Questions of morality and complicity only occur to him thanks to the efforts of his Jewish accountant Itzhak Stern (Ben Kingsley). Schindler saves Stern from deportation to the camps when he is arrested in the street without his work permit. Realizing how much influence Schindler has with the Nazi occupiers, Stern convinces him to hire ever more Jews as workers in his factory. Even when Stern is finally incarcerated in Plaszow, he and Schindler work to keep as many Jews as possible from being exterminated. Schindler establishes an uneasy agreement with Amon Goeth (Ralph Fiennes), the camp commandant. Re-establishing his factory (which now produces arms) within the camp itself, Schindler's actions work on two levels: the employment of whoever he can save (the list of the title), and the recalibration of machinery so that the munitions he manufactures are unusable.

Schindler and Stern's efforts, their desperation to preserve life, are juxtaposed throughout with the horrors of the concentration camp. Goeth, perched on the verandah of his villa above the camp, picking off men, women and children at random with a rifle, personifies the Nazi mindset that life — certainly non-Aryan life — is cheap. Images proliferate which bear testament to man's inhumanity to man: a child hides from his pursuers beneath a latrine, neck deep in effluent; bodies of murdered Jews are exhumed, piled up and set fire to, a Nazi officer discharging his pistol into the burning mound; beatings and shootings are ordered or administered by Goeth without a flicker of emotion.

For all the people that Schindler manages to save, the enormity of the Holocaust is brought home in the climactic scenes when Schindler, announcing to the inmates that a surrender has been effected and the war is over, then realizes that as a party member and an industrialist who has benefited from Nazi rule, he will have to go into hiding. Before he takes his leave, overcome at Stern's comradeship and resilience of spirit, Schindler breaks down, sobbing and blaming himself that he didn't do enough. Entirely the opposite is true, of course, but the sheer human cost of Nazi rule is brought unavoidably into focus in Schindler's despair.

Either because of subjective propagandist messaging, or reliance on action-packed pyrotechnic set pieces over realism, objectivity and verisimilitude are rarities as far as the cinematic treatment of World War II is concerned. For every determinedly unheroic anti-war film like *Cross of Iron* or *A Bridge Too Far* (Richard Attenborough, 1977), there is a slew of slam-bang blockbusting spectaculars that depict war as heroic, exciting, even fun.

Of Vietnam, the reverse is true. With the exception of *The Green Berets* (John Wayne/Ray Kellogg, 1968), whose pro-war sentiments are even more distasteful considering the conflict was still ongoing when it was made, every film that treats the subject has come out in protest of it. There are many notable Vietnam films — Oliver Stone's

Platoon (1986) and *Born on the Fourth of July* (1989), Stanley Kubrick's *Full Metal Jacket* (1987), Brian de Palma's *Casualties of War* (1989) – but two in particular represent towering and hugely influential works of cinema. One plunges its audience full-tilt into an almost psychedelic experience of the madness of war. The other bookends its shattering scenes of conflict and imprisonment with the before and the after, showing how people are changed, traumatized and destroyed by the horrors of a needless conflict.

Apocalypse Now (Francis Ford Coppola, 1979) starts in Saigon and ends in an encampment way 'up river', in Cambodia, where the renegade Colonel Kurtz (Marlon Brando) has gone native. Captain Willard (Martin Sheen), himself on the verge of a nervous breakdown, is ordered to seek out Kurtz and 'terminate with extreme prejudice'. Every stage of his odyssey by river (the film's literary template is Conrad's *Heart of Darkness*) takes him deeper into the madness of war. The clear-sighted anti-war aesthetic common to most intelligent films about World War I and II is here replaced by a more hallucinatory experience. War is hell, as the adage has it; in *Apocalypse Now*, war is more like a bad trip.

Willard first encounters the eccentric Colonel Kilgore (Robert Duvall), a man whose twin obsessions are surfing and Wagner, and who goes into battle wearing a ten-gallon hat. He leads a helicopter attack on a Vietnamese village, speakers blaring 'Ride of the Valkyries' ('scares the hell out of 'em'), for no other reason than the surfing opportunities presented by the river inlet that abuts the settlement. While the battle still rages, he quits his helicopter, strips off his combat fatigues and grabs his board, instructing an astounded young GI 'you can fight or you can surf'. His rationale – 'Charlie don't surf' – has passed into cinema history. Likewise his 'I love the smell of napalm in the morning' comment, occasioned when he recounts a previous operation, the day-long bombing of a suspected VC stronghold. 'We didn't find one of 'em, not one stinking dink body. But that smell, you know, that gasoline smell. The whole hill. Smelt like … victory.'

Willard witnesses any number of other incidents, reprehensible or outright ludicrous – from the gunning down of a Vietnamese family on a sampan (innocent victims of trigger-happy boat crew members Clean [Laurence Fishburne] and Chef [Frederic Forrest]) to a pointless battle over a bridge (shades of *The Good, the Bad and the Ugly*) – before finally confronting the absolutes of madness when he arrives at Kurtz's compound. Willard has come to feel some degree of empathy for Kurtz by this point and has been given to wonder about the validity of his mission. All doubts are soon removed.

At the compound – its bizarre, almost Andean temple surrounded by hanging bodies and heads on poles – Willard is greeted by a drug-fuelled photojournalist (Dennis Hopper), who venerates Kurtz as a prophet. Such gregariousness is not shared by Kurtz himself, who has his tribe of native followers subdue Willard and imprison him in a bamboo cage. He is obliged to listen to Kurtz's demented philosophizing (a stream of consciousness interlinked with fragments of T S Eliot), and is presented with the severed head of Chef. Eventually, Kurtz frees him. Willard avails himself of a machete and completes his mission. Kurtz's complicity transforms him, perversely, into an almost Christlike figure, with Willard as Judas, compelled to betray him; part of his grand design.

Willard's execution of Kurtz is intercut with a tribal ceremony where a caribou is hacked to pieces. As Willard emerges from the temple, Kurtz's followers gathered before him in silence, he throws down his machete. Similarly, they let drop their weapons, stepping aside as Willard walks through them, back to the boat. The anti-violence implication of this scene, tribalism robbed of its savagery at the death of the leader, is emphasized as Kurtz's final words echo in Willard's ears as he leaves the compound: 'The horror … the horror.'

The Deer Hunter (Michael Cimino, 1978) starts and ends in Pennsylvania, where harsh conditions are taken for granted. The steel

At gunpoint: Nick (Christopher Walken) is forced into a deadly game in *The Deer Hunter*

126

mills which provide employment are like something out of Hieronymous Bosch; leisure time is spent in the mountains, rifle in hand, hunting. Taking the deer with one shot is a matter of honour, the business of death conducted with greater care and attention to detail than the business of steel. But it is not until the scene switches to Vietnam that the reality of death – and the appalling devaluation of life – becomes clear.

Lifelong friends Michael (Robert de Niro) and Nick (Christopher Walken) volunteer for the army. In a telling scene at a wedding reception, they drunkenly venerate a soldier, raising their glasses and bragging that they are about to ship out. The man cannot even bring himself to respond, but his face communicates such a potent mixture of pity and contempt that no words are necessary. Whatever their motivations for signing up – patriotism; escape from a small town and a dead-end life – their experience of war soon disabuses them of any valiant notions. And worse awaits them when they are captured.

Incarcerated in bamboo cages partially submerged in a filthy brown river, they are subjected, initially, to psychological violence: the discomfort of their prison, the constant barrage of voices speaking a language they can't understand – voices raised in anger. Shots are heard, as are screams. One soldier breaks down even before he's questioned: he is transferred to a cage that is almost totally submerged and overrun with rats.

For those who are questioned, it soon becomes clear that the acquisition of information is not particularly high on the Viet Cong's list of priorities. Interrogations degenerate into enforced games of Russian roulette. Michael and Nick are made to sit opposite each other, kept at gunpoint and encouraged by frequent slaps to the face. They take it in turns pulling the trigger, barrel jammed hard against their temple, as the VC eagerly place bets.

The escalation of the game, Michael urging their captors to load the chamber with three bullets, presents an opportunity for escape. He and Nick again take turns: empty chambers. Sure of a couple of good shots, he turns the pistol on the guards, quickly grabbing a machine gun from the first one to fall. Nick does the same. The catharsis of their retribution is undeniable, although Nick becomes manic, repeatedly bludgeoning an already incapacitated VC with the stock of the rifle.

Their escape is simply a gateway to further trauma. Michael, who makes it back to America, finds that his only other friend from the Army, Steven (John Savage), is confined to a wheelchair in a veterans' institution; his life is no life at all. Michael has problems reintegrating into civilian life. Reunited with fellow steelworkers on a deer hunt, he pulls a gun on the petulant Stan (John Cazale) after a dispute. The madness of Vietnam is thus brought back home.

For Nick, it is worse. At the fall of Saigon, he is still there – disturbed, amnesiac and unable to comprehend his actions – earning money in the back rooms of seedy bars. Playing Russian roulette. Michael makes a risky return journey in order to rescue his friend from himself. When Nick doesn't recognize him, Michael ventures into even more dangerous territory, taking his turn opposite Nick, hoping the sight of him with a gun to his head will spark his friend's memory. It doesn't and he is fortunate that the hammer falls on an empty chamber. Nick is not so lucky; he seizes the gun immediately Michael has set it down and before he can be stopped pulls the trigger on a live round.

We have seen, then, that war films have great potency in depicting man's inhumanity to man (not to mention the painful aftermath) and the cruelties inflicted in times of conflict. These films are also about sides, division: Nazis/Jews in *Schindler's List*, Viet Cong/Americans in *The Deer Hunter*, etc. 'Take off one uniform and there's always another one underneath,' says Steiner in *Cross of Iron*. It's an acute remark in a film which demonstrates that the danger a professional soldier faces isn't always from the so-called enemy. *Cross of Iron* is about division within the same regiment, based on the hierarchy of rank; it is not just an anti-war film, but also an anti-military one.

Anti-militarism and criticism of the officer classes often centre on disciplinary excesses and court-martials. **The Hill** (Sidney Lumet, 1965) is set in a camp where military prisoners – 'the dodgy boys, the spivs, the cowards, the thieves, the weak chain in the system' – are punished, broken down and remoulded as disciplined soldiers. At least such is the aim of RSM Wilson (Harry Andrews). Wilson is a strict disciplinarian. His adjutant and protégé, Williams (Ian Hendry), is just a sadist. Conflict occurs when five new prisoners are transferred to the camp, their number including Joe Roberts (Sean Connery), on a charge for physically assaulting a superior officer who ordered him into a certain-death situation, McGrath (Jack Watson), arrested for drunken brawling, and Jacko King (Ossie Davis), singled out for no other reason than being black. They are billeted in a cell with the petulant Bartlett (Roy Kinnear) and a good-natured family man, George Stevens (Alfred Lynch). Wilson responds to the insubordination of these internees by making them take the hill, a fifty-foot construction of rocks and sand, which they are forced to climb at the double in full pack and uniform, turning about face once they reach the bottom on the opposite side and scaling it again.

Wilson leaves them to Williams's not-so-tender mercies. Williams, determined to carve himself a reputation for sternness and thereby step out of Wilson's shadow, is over-zealous in his attitude to punishment. Stevens dies as a direct result. Roberts incites a riot, which Wilson quells. But Roberts insists on making a complaint against Williams. Aggrieved, but still confident he can beat the rap, Williams offers Roberts the chance to go man to man in a solitary confinement cell. Roberts takes him up on it, but at the last moment Williams signals for two guards to follow

Joe Roberts (Sean Connery) stands up against authority in *The Hill*

him in. They give Roberts a thorough working over. Dumped back in his cell, face bruised, this affront motivates King and McGrath to come out in support of him.

A power struggle ensues. The prisoners, hitherto played off against each other, form an alliance with the camp's only two humanitarian officers Harris (Ian Bannen) and the medical orderly (Michael Redgrave) who announce that they will bring charges against Williams. Wilson, finally realizing that his adjutant is using him, leaves him to face the flak. But the prisoners' victory over their nemesis is short-lived. When Williams, cornering the injured Roberts in his cell, makes threatening overtures, McGrath and King step in. 'Don't mess him up,' Roberts implores them, 'we've won.' But reason is lost on them. The last shot is an anguished close-up of Roberts's face as Williams's screams fill the soundtrack.

Joseph Losey's bitterly titled **King and Country** (1964) is set in the trenches of Passchendaele in 1917 and details the trial for desertion of an enlisted man, Private Hamp (Tom Courtenay). He is defended by Captain Hargreaves (Dirk Bogarde), a middle-class officer whose pompous worldview and self-serving rhetoric are challenged by the simple-minded but fundamentally decent Hamp.

The only survivor of the platoon he joined at the outbreak of war, Hamp has endured three years of misery, entrenched, almost continually under fire, and one day he simply walks away from his post. Captured and confined to a cell, he awaits trial. As Hargreaves becomes increasingly emotionally involved, his chances of winning Hamp's case grow less and less likely. Hamp does himself little favour; under cross-examination from the prosecution, he repeats parrot-fashion phrases Hargreaves has instructed him to use. Asked why he has given such answers, he replies with embarrassingly gauche honesty, 'Because Captain Hargreaves said to.'

He is, of course, found guilty. High command, whose jurisdiction would allow the imposition of a more lenient sentence, decree that he is to be shot, citing as their reason the 'morale' of Hamp's fellow soldiers, due to go over the top again very shortly. This concept of 'morale' as a synonym for fear, or for a warning, strengthens *King and Country*'s anti-war credentials. (It is worth mentioning that the film does not contain any scenes of battle or enemy engagement; the only violence we see onscreen is that done by the British Army against one of its own.)

Hamp passes a comfortless night prior to his execution. He is billeted with the bluntly pragmatic Private Sparrow (Jeremy Spenser), who tells him, 'It doesn't matter who kills you now, does it? ... You rot in the mud and that's that. Doesn't matter what anyone bloody well thinks about it, does it? ... We'll all be rat food before much longer.'

Hamp's death is as gruelling as Sparrow's ghoulish little soliloquy suggests. He is strapped to a chair and carried, blindfolded, in front of the firing squad. A fusillade of shots rings out. Justice has failed Hamp, and so too do his executioners prove themselves failures. He is badly, but not fatally, wounded. It is left to Hargreaves to finish the job. He avails himself of a pistol, goes warily over to where Hamp lies bleeding. He lifts the young man's head:

Hargreaves: Isn't it finished yet?
Hamp: No, sir. I'm sorry.

On this truly pitiful note, Hargreaves ends Hamp's life – and as he pulls the trigger, one feels he might as well be ending his own.

Even more pointless is the court-martial in **Paths of Glory** (Kubrick, 1957). The setting is again the World War I. The maniacal and arrogant General Mireau (George Macready) orders an offensive against a strongly defended enemy position, nicknamed the Ant Hill. When the battle ends in heavy losses and an inevitable retreat, he accepts no blame for it, insisting that the troops did not fight hard enough. He furthermore decrees that three randomly selected soldiers shall be shot for cowardice as 'an example'. The first half of the film, then, shows human life wasted on a grand scale in the assault on the Ant Hill (a target which has little strategic merit – any victory would only have been symbolic). The second shows the same thing, but on a smaller, more intimate scale – and to even less avail.

The line of fire: the inhumanity of execution in *Paths of Glory*

At the court-martial the scapegoats are defended by the idealistic Colonel Dax (Kirk Douglas) who, before the war, had been a criminal lawyer. Although he uncovers evidence of conspiracy and professional ineptitude among the high command, he is powerless to prevent Mireau and his fellow officer General Broulard (Adolphe Menjou) from seeing the execution through. The trial is a kangaroo court, and even with his legal experience in civilian life, Dax's efforts prove as futile as Hargreaves's and the threesome are executed. One of them, unable to walk and barely conscious, is strapped to a board (like Hamp to his chair) and carted out in front of the firing squad. The scene is played out to a militaristic drumming, a reminder that like Travis in *If...*, Gittes in *Chinatown* and McMurphy in *One Flew Over the Cuckoo's Nest*, this is the age-old story of the individual against the system.

Anti-militarism for the Vietnam generation comes courtesy of ***First Blood*** (Ted Kofcheff, 1982), adapted from David Morrell's novel. Clouded with a reputation it doesn't deserve thanks to tabloid hysteria (see chapter four) and two exploitative sequels, the film is actually clear-sighted in its criticism of violence. Its simple uncluttered narrative concerns a manhunt launched by Will Teasle (Brian Dennehy), a heavy-handed sheriff. His quarry is John Rambo (Sylvester Stallone), a former Green Beret and holder of the congressional medal of honour, traumatized by the tortures he suffered in captivity in Vietnam, and (like Michael in *The Deer Hunter*) unable to re-adjust to civilian life. The difference, however, is that Rambo was never going to be able to function in a non-military environment. Trained and deployed by the quixotic Colonel Trautman (Richard Crenna), his role in the war was little more than a killing machine. 'In the Army ... I was in charge of million-dollar equipment,' he says at one point; 'now I can't even get a job washing cars.'

It is Rambo's non-belonging in society that leads him into conflict with Teasle. A drifter, long-haired and unshaven, he is hitching through a small town when Teasle picks him up and makes it clear that 'guys like you' are unwelcome. (The irony, that Teasle has taken him for a hippie or delinquent, is compounded when Rambo recollects the scene at the airport when he came back from Vietnam, long-haired protestors 'spitting, calling me "baby-killer"'.) Although Teasle cites his crime as vagrancy ('that's gonna look good on his grave at Arlington', Trautman sneers), all Rambo does is defy the older man by walking back into town when Teasle deposits him at the town limits and tells him to keep on walking. Arrested, maltreated at the police headquarters (where he suffers flashbacks), he overcomes his captors and escapes. Heading into the mountains outside of town, his military and survivalist skills snap back into place, and he begins to turn the tables on his pursuers.

The generational difference between Rambo and Teasle emphasizes that the violence in *First Blood* stems from social prejudice (re-united with Trautman for the first time since Vietnam, Rambo tells him that their code of honour doesn't exist in civilian life – 'there are no friendly civilians,' he opines). And the system – the establishment – has just as much to answer for as society. The Army has 'created' him: 'trained to ignore pain, to ignore weather,' as Trautman puts it, adding that his orders were 'when in doubt, kill'. Authority (in the form of a small town sheriff) has persecuted him. Teasle comes across as a forerunner of 'Little' Bill in *Unforgiven*, a man who just wants his town free of lawlessness, but whose methods are brutal and misguided. When the manhunt intensifies, Teasle's men joined by state troopers and the National Guard, the metaphor is clear: small town America as a microcosm of military involvement in Vietnam. And when, in the explosive finale[5], Rambo lays waste to the town, the war quite literally comes home. Indeed, the film is so focused on these concerns that it is difficult to understand the ethos – right-wing and pro-military – that infuses its sequels.

coda

The events of 11 September 2001 were devastating and far-reaching. Television images of the attack on the twin towers of the World Trade Center have been seen the world over. These images are indelibly etched on the consciousness of a generation. They do not need to be dwelt upon in any detail in this book.

Hollywood's immediate response reflected concern over cinematic representation of New York's now irrevocably altered skyline in forthcoming releases. A 'teaser' trailer (i.e. one featuring footage not necessarily analogous to the narrative of the actual movie) for Sam Raimi's *Spider-Man*, which showed a helicopter entangled in a web spun between the two towers, was withdrawn. Poster artwork for Rod Lurie's *The Last Castle* and Edward Burns's *Sidewalks of New York* were re-designed. Indeed, *Sidewalks of New York*, a low-budget romantic comedy, was subjected to the same release date postponement that befell the likes of *Collateral Damage*, a Schwarzenegger thriller about terrorism, and Barry Sonnenfeld's *Big Trouble*, in which lax security allows a bomb to be smuggled into an airport.

In the UK, **Swordfish** (Dominic Sena, 2001) was pulled from distribution. A slick mainstream production centring on hi-tech criminality, its undertones of terrorism are used, in a manner not dissimilar to *Die Hard*, as something of a red herring to obfuscate what is essentially a heist thriller. Nonetheless, the opening scene was deemed contentious. Master criminal Gabriel Shear (John Travolta) takes over a federal bank, holding staff and employees hostage. The hostages are compelled to wear explosive devices electronically rigged to detonate should they traverse a certain radius. A SWAT team effect counter measures, shooting one of Shear's men and 'rescuing' the young woman he was holding at gunpoint. Despite her protestations, they haul her away from the bank. True to Shear's warnings, the device is triggered, the C4 plastic explosive layered with ball bearings which explode outwards in all directions. Hostage and SWAT team are killed outright, and an entire city block is laid to waste.

Swordfish's withdrawal is understandable. Even now, the scene is uncomfortable to watch. Indeed, in the aftermath of 11 September, a number of films become uneasy to watch, so prescient is their imagery. The tower blocks exploding at the end of *Fight Club* is a case in point; or the vision of fallen skyscrapers in a waterlogged Manhattan in Spielberg's *A.I.* (2001).

There are, of course, other films whose plots and narrative concerns prefigured the tragic events, if anything even more explicitly than *Fight Club* or *A.I.* Looking back through a decade of action thrillers, one realizes that with the end of the Cold War, Hollywood's search for a new all-purpose villain shifted from communism to the arena of terrorist activity. While political terrorism (usually represented by the IRA) is the mainstay of such films as *Patriot Games* (Phillip Noyce, 1992) and *The Devil's Own* (Alan J Pakula, 1997), studios have garnered richer pickings from religious (usually Islamic) fanaticism. Divorced from strictly political ends, driven by a suicidal hatred of the West, the paranoia factor has routinely been exploited: consider *True Lies* (Cameron, 1994), *The Peacemaker* (Mimi Leder, 1997), *The Siege* (Ed Zwick, 1999).

Perhaps the most predictive entry in this genre is **Executive Decision** (Stuart Baird, 1996). Met with critical indifference on its release, it is a fairly standard action film following an elite counter-terrorist team led by Kurt Russell as they attempt to board a hijacked airliner and defuse a bomb before the flight passes the point at which it can be shot down by the military without causing civilian injuries on the ground, an act of containment requiring the presidential authorization to which the title refers. What makes *Executive Decision* an unsettling film to watch now is the ease with which the terrorists take over the flight, and their intention of using a passenger jet as a suicide bomb. Shorn of its race-against-time heroics and the political dilemma of whether or not to shoot down the plane before it reaches its target, the film's plot is unnervingly prophetic.

Kurt Russell and Halle Berry in *Executive Decision*

Of course, *Executive Decision* was made five years before the events mirrored in its basic scenario. In the wake of 11 September, studios shelved or moved back release dates for a number of projects dealing with similar subjects. Hollywood has always leaned towards the darker and more violent aspects of the human psyche in order to centralize the conflicts between its heroes and villains – one thinks of the perennial popularity of the war, crime and horror genres – but following the terrorist attacks on New York, there was a sense of re-evaluation.

It is in such a climate that an analysis of violence in cinema becomes more acute, less easy to treat glibly or ironically. The very morality of film violence comes under scrutiny. This book began with an evaluation of Clint Eastwood's contribution to the western, and Eastwood has certainly succeeded in communicating a message of anti-violence in *The Outlaw Josey Wales* and *Unforgiven*; however, this has come at the cost of an iconic, amoral 'hard man' image cultivated in other genre films – westerns such as *A Fistful of Dollars*, *Joe Kidd* and *High Plains Drifter*,

135

and thrillers such as *Dirty Harry*, *The Eiger Sanction* and *Tightrope*.

As with Eastwood, the violence in the films of Martin Scorsese is graphic and realistic, yet there is very much a social/moral context to it. On the other hand, there are Tarantino and his imitators, who deal unashamedly in 'movie' violence, purely for reasons of iconography and entertainment.

The issue of violence as entertainment leads us to the question of responsibility. Whereas the likes of the Bond films are utterly divorced from reality through their exotic locations, glamorous and larger-than-life characters, expensive milieus (flash cars, casinos) and hi-tech gadgetry, there is still cause for concern over mainstream productions which package designer violence in MTV-style visuals and trendy soundtracks, marketed at impressionable teenage audiences.

And what of films such as *Fight Club* or *Falling Down*, which trade on social angst? Although *Fight Club* kicks against the mainstream, it still delivers a large quota of iconic moments, not to mention an enunciation of disaffection against an increasingly corporate and materialistic society that many of us can empathize with, even if we don't actually go to the lengths Tyler Durden does in his rebellion against homogeny and consumerism. Despite its undertones of social satire, *Fight Club* sends out a potent message, and one wonders how many teens and twenty-somethings found in it a mirror for their own disenchantment.

Similarly, the morality of *Falling Down* is blurred. The innocent bystanders killed in the drive-by shooting are not dwelt upon; the middle-class buffoon on the golf course, while obtrusive, certainly doesn't deserve to die. D-Fens's last line – 'I'm the bad guy?' – accentuates the sense of ambiguity that pervades the entire film. The shifts in tone between social comment and black comedy (almost, at times, verging on slapstick) leave one wondering what point Schumacher is making. Ambiguity has the potential to be a dangerous thing in this type of film, as it allows the social or moral implications to go uncommunicated to audience members who might instead focus on the iconography or black humour.

Ideally, as with *American History X*, a film dealing with violence and the effects of violence should have a duty to consider its subject matter from as many angles and with as little hyperbole as possible. Social conscience should be foremost in mind.

Ultimately, how a film is perceived will always remain a matter of personal aesthetics on the part of each audience member, while the issue of what is justified in being shown on screen (and for what reasons) remains the responsibility of the filmmaker.

NOTES

CHAPTER ONE: INFLUENCE AND ICONOGRAPHY

1 The Sixties saw a proliferation of westerns shot cheaply in Europe by Italian or Spanish directors, usually with an American star in the lead role and indigenous actors filling out the rest of the cast. Known as 'spaghetti westerns', Leone's opuses were the most well-known and widely distributed. Other notable films include *Django* and *A Professional Gun* (both by Sergio Corbucci), and Damiano Damiani's *A Bullet for the General*.

2 World cinema has exerted a profound influence on the American mainstream, most notably in terms of remakes. Kurosawa's masterpiece *The Seven Samurai* was remade as *The Magnificent Seven*, while *The Hidden Fortress* provided the blueprint for *Star Wars*.

3 Political considerations would play an even greater part in Leone's next film, *A Fistful of Dynamite*, a blackly comic revolutionary fable.

4 And back again, since Woo now works in Hollywood.

5 Empire, issue 146 (August 2001).

6 A clip of Woo's *A Better Tomorrow 2* is used in Tony Scott's *True Romance* (scripted by Tarantino).

7 Maitland McDonagh, 'Broken Mirrors, Broken Minds: the Dark Dreams of Dario Argento' (Sun Tavern Fields, 1991), p.23.

8 The most famous of which, *Ocean's 11* (Lewis Milestone, 1960), was remade in 2002 by Steven Soderbergh.

CHAPTER TWO: TAKING IT TO THE LIMIT

1 Hitchcock's use of Freudian imagery was seldom subtle. *North by Northwest*, the psychological subtext of which concerns a man whose journey through life is hampered by mother figures, ends with its hero, liberated, clambering into bed with an attractive blonde; Hitchcock immediately cuts to a train thundering into a tunnel.

2 Tarantino's setting of the scene, letting the audience's imagination do the work, has its precursor in *Kiss Me Deadly* (Aldrich, 1955). When the luckless heroine Velda (Maxine Cooper) is tortured, all that Aldrich shows us is a close-up of a pair of pliers, followed by her legs, dangling from the end of a bed, twitching as she screams. Two brief shots. But the implication is repulsive.

3 Richard has qualms about killing an enemy soldier in the line of fire, but doesn't blink at going AWOL to pursue a personal vendetta.

4 It has also been released as *Day of the Woman*.

5 Camille Keaton was the grandniece of silent movie comedy star Buster Keaton.

6 This kind of scene – sex as a prelude to death – became a staple of the genre. In Wes Craven's *Scream*, one of the characters, discoursing on the conventions of horror movies, says, 'You can never have sex – it's one of the rules.' (The exception, of course, is *The Wicker Man*.)

7 Fukasaku's use of classical music – Verdi's 'Requiem', Johann Strauss's 'Radetsky March' and Johann Strauss II's 'Blue Danube Waltz' all feature prominently – recalls Kubrick's in *A Clockwork Orange* and Coppola's in *Apocalypse Now*. As with these films, the effect is contrapuntal and heightens the audience's emotional awareness of the onscreen depiction of violence.

CHAPTER THREE: AMORALITY AND ANTI-HEROISM

1 Huston had co-scripted *High Sierra* with W R Burnett, from Burnett's own novel.

2 William Ernest Henley, 'Invictus', line 7.

3 Coppola's completion of the saga twenty years later, *The Godfather Part III*, has Michael Corleone seeking atonement for his sins and legitimacy for the Corleone family. He fails on both counts: further conflict with his peers in the underworld culminates in the death of his daughter by an assassin's bullet meant for him. At the end of the film he dies alone.

4 These lines are spoken by Scorsese himself.

5 A piece of witty casting here. Ten years earlier, Vincent played Salvy, the unfortunate who gets beaten half to death by Pesci, his head slammed by a car door, in Scorsese's *Raging Bull*.

6 *Manhunter*'s credits refer to him as 'Dr Lecktor'. For the sake of continuity, however, I have referred to the character throughout as 'Lecter' (this spelling is consistent in Thomas Harris's novels).

7 The music is J S Bach's 'Goldberg Variations'. The same piece plays on Lecter's portable cassette recorder while he kills his guards in *The Silence of the Lambs*.

8 The ending of Harris's novel, derided by many critics, has Lecter and Starling embark upon a relationship. The film's denouement retains the romantic element that makes *Hannibal* a very different work from its predecessors, but also seems somewhat narratively unsatisfying.

9 *Licence to Kill* (John Glen, 1989).

10 The relationship between unionism and crime is well documented in America, most notably in the case of Teamsters leader Jimmy Hoffa and his connections with the Mafia. Hoffa was the subject of the eponymous 1992 film directed by Danny de Vito.

11 Bickle's disturbed persona has its real-life counterpart in John Hinckley, whose obsession with Jodie Foster became public after his attempt to assassinate Ronald Reagan.

12 The film is also known as *Angel of Vengeance*.

CHAPTER FOUR: CENSORSHIP AND CONTROVERSY

1 It had already been applied to one case, merely days before the Hungerford massacre, when Julian Knight shot and killed six people in Melbourne,

Australia, and would have committed suicide had he not run out of ammunition. The press described him as a 'Rambo Sniper'.

2 NC-17 means that no children under 17 are permitted to watch the film, as opposed to an R rating, where children younger than 17 can gain access to the film when accompanied by an adult. NC-17 is considered persona non grata in Hollywood, and is unconducive to box-office takings as certain publications will not run advertisements for films carrying the NC-17 rating.

3 Notwithstanding his draconian image, Ferman was openly supportive of the film. As Empire reported at the time, 'Ferman…considers the film to be an important piece of work, even going so far as to invite Stone to the board's London office to talk to him about it' (Empire, issue 67, January 1995).

4 David Kerekes and David Slater, *See No Evil: Banned Films and Video Controversy* (Critical Vision/Headpress, 2000), p.325.

5 Vincent LoBrotto, *Stanley Kubrick* (Faber & Faber, 1997), p.369.

6 Much of which is reputed to have been shot by Steven Spielberg, billed on the credits as co-writer and producer.

7 Similar scenes/iconography occur in *I Spit on Your Grave* and *The Texas Chain Saw Massacre*, indication of the influence *Last House on the Left* had on genre cinema in the Seventies.

8 Co-director Trinh Thi, as well as both of her lead actresses, worked in hardcore features.

CHAPTER FIVE: NO FAREWELL TO ARMS

1 This device is reminiscent of Ruggero Deodato's infamous *Cannibal Holocaust* (1979), which charts the efforts of a team of documentarists to track down a tribe of cannibals. The final shot has the cameraman abandoning his equipment only for his death, seconds later, to be recorded on it.

2 Other contemporized reworkings of this sub-genre include Carpenter's earlier *Assault on Precinct* 13 (1976) and Peckinpah's *Straw Dogs*.

3 The bikers are led by special effects maestro Tom Savini. His swarthy iconic presence has also netted him acting roles in Romero's *Knightriders* (1981) and Robert Rodriguez's *From Dusk Till Dawn* (1996).

4 Even his name is a mark of disrespect to traditional American values.

5 It should be noted that despite the amount of destruction in the finale (a gas station is blown up and several buildings shot to pieces), the only victim of Rambo's attack on the town is Teasle himself – and he is seen being attended to by ambulance personnel, still alive, in the closing scenes. By comparison, David Morrell's exceptional novel is considerably more violent, ending with the deaths of both of its main characters.

SELECTED BIBLIOGRAPHY

The author is indebted to the following publications:

Baker, Rick and Russell, Toby *The Essential Guide to Hong Kong Movies* (Eastern Heroes Publications, 1994)

Baxter, John *Stanley Kubrick: A Biography* (HarperCollins, 1997)

Biskind, Peter *Easy Riders Raging Bulls* (Bloomsbury, 1998)

Chibnall, Steve and Murphy, Robert, eds. *British Crime Cinema* (Routledge, 1999)

Kerekes, David and Slater, David *See No Evil: Banned Films and Video Controversy* (Critical Vision/Headpress, 2000)

LoBrutto, Vincent *Stanley Kubrick* (Faber & Faber, 1997)

McDonagh, Maitland *Broken Mirrors, Broken Minds: the Dark Dreams of Dario Argento* (Sun Tavern Fields, 1991)

Palmer, James and Riley, Michael *The Films of Joseph Losey* (Cambridge University Press, 1993)

Rodley, Chris, ed. *Cronenberg on Cronenberg* (Faber & Faber, 1992)

Thompson, David and Christie, Ian , eds. *Scorsese on Scorsese* (Faber & Faber, 1989)

Empire, issue 67 (January 1995), editorial, '*Natural Born Killers*: The Story So Far'

Empire, issue 146 (August 2001), 'The Name Above the Title', by Liz Beardsworth and Ian Freer

ACKNOWLEDGEMENTS

My thanks to the following for permission to quote from copyright materials: Critical Vision/Headpress for *See No Evil: Banned Films and Video Controversy* by David Kerekes and David Slater. Faber & Faber for *Stanley Kubrick* by Vincent LoBrutto. Empire for excerpts from the articles '*Natural Born Killers*: The Story So Far' and 'The Name Above the Title'.

Thanks to Tina Persaud at B T Batsford for her continued support.

A mention in dispatches to the following: my Mother and Father, Viv and Dennis Apple, Michael Eaton, Martin and Glenda Holroyd, Mandy Morrell and the 'Mild Bunch', Carole Parnell, the 'usual suspects' at the NWC, and my friends and colleagues at The Classical Music Shop.

Finally, a large vote of thanks to Paul Rowe for his advice and input on this book.

APPENDIX

List of films compiled by the Department of Public Prosecutions in July 1984 as suitable for prosecution under the Obscene Publications Act 1959. An asterisk indicates those that have since been certificated for video, albeit in edited versions.

Absurd (Peter Newton [i.e. Aristide Massaccesi], 1981)
Anthropophagus, the Beast (Joe D'Amato [i.e. Aristide Massaccesi], 1980)
Axe (Frederick R Friedel, 1974)
The Beast in Heat (Ivan Katansky [i.e. Luigi Batzella], 1977)
Blood Bath, a.k.a. *Bay of Blood* (Mario Bava, 1971)★
Blood Feast (Herschell Gordon Lewis, 1963)
Blood Rites (Andy Milligan, 1967)
Bloody Moon (Jesus Franco, 1981)
The Burning (Tony Maylam, 1980)★
Cannibal Apocalypse (Anthony M Dawson [i.e. Antonio Margheriti], 1980)
Cannibal Ferox (Umberto Lenzi, 1981)★
Cannibal Holocaust (Ruggero Deodato, 1979)
The Cannibal Man (Eloy de la Iglesia, 1972)★
Devil Hunter (Clifford Brown [i.e. Jesus Franco], 1980)
Don't Go Into the Woods Alone (James Bryan, 1980)
The Driller Killer (Abel Ferrara, 1979)★
Evilspeak (Eric Weston, 1981)
Exposé (James Kenelm Clarke, 1975)
Faces of Death (Conan la Cilare, 1979)
Fight For Your Life (Robert A Endelson, 1977)
Forest of Fear (Charles McCrann, 1978)
Frankenstein, i.e. *Andy Warhol's Frankenstein* (Paul Morrissey, 1973)
Gestapo's Last Orgy (Cesare Canevari, 1977)
The House by the Cemetery (Lucio Fulci, 1981)★
House on the Edge of the Park (Ruggero Deodato, 1980)
I Spit on Your Grave (Meir Zarchi, 1978)★
Island of Death (Nico Mastorakis, 1972)
The Last House on the Left (Wes Craven, 1972)
Love Camp 7 (R L Frost, 1968)
Madhouse (Ovidio G Assonitis, 1981)
Mardi Gras Massacre (Jack Weis, 1978)
Nightmares in a Damaged Brain (Romano Scavolini, 1981)★
Night of the Bloody Apes (René Cardona, 1968)
Night of the Demon (James C Wasson, 1980)
Snuff (director not credited, 1971)
SS Experiment Camp (Sergio Garrone, 1976)
Tenebrae (Dario Argento, 1982)★
The Werewolf and the Yeti (Miguel Iglesias Bonns, 1975)
Zombie Flesh Eaters (Lucio Fulci, 1979)★

INDEX

Page numbers in italics
denote illustrations

144